Standing
in the Gap

An initiative of God

INTERCESSORY
PRAYERS

Henry R. Darko

7905 N Crescent Blvd
Pennsauken, NJ 08110

Unless otherwise indicated, I took all Scripture quotations in this book from the King James Version (KJV) of the Holy Bible.

Standing in the Gap

Copyright © 2022 by Henry R. Darko

For information, contact:

Published by
BookBaby7905 N Crescent Blvd
Pennsauken, NJ 08110
https://www.bookbaby.com

Cover design by the Author
Contribution and Edited by AD Darko
Edited by Prof. Dr. Astronaut

ISBN: 978-1-66788-162-1

DEDICATION

I dedicate this book to the Almighty God, for instituting intercession for the sinful man's restoration for His glory.

CONTENTS

ACKNOWLEDGMENTS

I give all the glory and honor to the Almighty God for the beautiful things He has done in my life. By His grace and mercy alone, I began and completed this project. I am also grateful to my Savior and High Priest, Jesus Christ, who is always interceding for me. Also, I cannot forget the daily guidance of the Holy Spirit. I honor you, Jehovah, for the strength and wisdom to author this book.

I also appreciate my wife, Ama. She gave me great feedback and encouraged me to complete this project.

Finally, I am grateful to my beautiful children, who inspire me to do my best in everything I do. God bless you.

Introduction

Standing in the gap means praying for someone to receive God's mercy for restoration (Ezekiel 22:30). When Adam and Eve disobeyed God's laws by eating the forbidden fruit in the Garden, they lost their dominion, fellowship, and communion with Him. The rebellion led to the fall of man and separation from God, marking the beginning of misery for humanity (Genesis 3). But God knew this, so He foreordained Jesus, the High Priest, as our ultimate intercessor. Later, Jesus manifested as the divine sacrificial Lamb, slain from the foundation of the world to intercede for our redemption and restoration (1 Peter 1: 18-21; Revelation. 12:8).

God **initiates** and determines **who, what, when, how, and where** to intercede for His glory. Before Jesus arrived, God established covenants with godly people.

- **Enoch** and **Noah**, after Adam's rebellion.
- As men prospered and increased in numbers, the cycle of disobedience continued. For example, the wickedness and rebellion of Sodom and Gomorrah attracted God's judgment, but He found **Abraham** faithful and established a covenant with him.

Abraham's prayer for Sodom and Gomorrah was the first intercession recorded in the Bible. God conferred the covenant promises from Abraham upon his son **Isaac** and his grandson **Jacob** (Gen 18, 26-28).

The descendants of Jacob's twelve sons became the Israelites enslaved in Egypt. After four hundred and thirty years, God commissioned **Moses** as a prophet to lead Israel from bondage in Egypt to the Promised Land of Canaan (Exodus 3:1-18). Moses was a great intercessor for the Israelites during their forty-year journey to Canaan.

- God established a covenant with the Israelites that they would obey His laws and He would bless them. He designated **Aaron** and **his descendants** from the tribe of Levi as priests who ministered to Him. They were to teach and practice the covenant laws. God also directed the priests to intercede and atone for Israel's sins with the blood of animals.

The Priests performed their duties excellently. With time, they defied the law and profaned the sacred with idolatry, showing no reverence for God by offering imperfect sacrifices. They maltreated their wives and widows and neglected the less privileged in their midst. Besides extortion and robbery, they exploited the foreign residents without justice, deceived the people, and led Israel astray. So, God rejected their prayers. The priest sullied their duties and failed in this noble service.

Thus, God's judgment came upon them. For instance, He punished Eli, the high priest, and his sons, for defiling the offering and sacrifice. God honored those who obeyed His Word (1 Sam. 2). So He chose the tribe of Judah and established His covenant with the lineage of **David** in Israel. Two Kingdoms emerged after Solomon's demise, the North Israel and the South, Judah. Israel later backslid and served idols.

Like the backsliding Israel, Judah gradually turned their back on God and committed idolatry. They also despised the Sabbath, made alliances, and sought help from Egypt that violated the law. Judah became a people of sin and iniquity, squandering the rights God gave them.

- Therefore, God used prophets like **Isaiah** and **Jeremiah** to warn Judah about their rebellion and preach repentance to avert Israel's impending destruction.

However, when Judah refused to heed God's further warning, they became victims of Babylonian captivity and went into exile. Yet, God restored a remnant of Judah because of His covenant with David. Even in captivity, prophets like Ezekiel and Daniel interceded for the restoration of Judah. Although God used prophets to preach repentance for revival in Israel, the revivals were short-lived because the people returned to their wickedness after enjoying freedom, and the intercessor died. Also, animal blood could not accomplish man's salvation, nor change the sinful inner being.

Later, God manifested in the flesh as Jesus and offered Himself for man on the cross. He anointed and empowered Jesus with the Holy Spirit for His earthly ministry (Luke 4:18).

Jesus interceded for others during His ministry while on Earth.
- He healed the sick, set the captives free, and delivered some from demons.
- He fulfilled His ultimate mandate when He interceded and paid the ultimate price for man's sins with His blood.

Jesus became the **ultimate intercessor** because He set humanity free from the bondage of sin and reconciled man to God. This the blood of animals could not accomplish (Romans 3:25). The sacrifice of Jesus on the cross nullified the need for animal sacrifices and burned offerings. Thus, God's presence became accessible to all who believe in His Son, Jesus Christ. Jesus prayed according to His Father's will without compromising the truth and interceded for all men, including those who hated and persecuted Him.

Thus, God gave Him a name above all names for His obedience. Jesus now sits at God's right hand, interceding for humanity (Philippians 2:6-11). He made all believers in Him priests to proclaim His message and intercede for others, unlike the anointed few who could pray to God for Israel in the Old Testament (1 Peter 2:4-10). Jesus is the only way to the Father, so we pray to God through Him (John 14:6). His Apostles interceded in the name of Jesus as they preached the gospel. They showed compassion and never demanded rewards from the people for intercessory prayers. God also provided all their needs as He rewards faithfulness to His Word in the vineyard.

God empowers every believer with the Holy Spirit as our helper, comforter, counselor, advocate, and intercessor through Jesus. He also endowed believers with gifts of the Holy Spirit. These include words of wisdom, healing, miracles, faith, and the discerning of spirits to benefit everyone. He convicts our sinful hearts, leads us to repentance, and grants us righteousness, resulting in a personal relationship with God through Jesus Christ. Once saved after repentance, Jesus lives in our hearts as a seal of our eternal inheritance. Also, The Holy Spirit teaches the Word and helps us pray according to God's will. He helps us to produce the fruits of love, faith, peace, joy, compassion, patience, and obedience.

This book intends to draw your attention to the relevance of intercessory prayers for God's mercy and restoration. It contrasts how the Old Testament seasonal animal sacrifice for intercession was a shadow of the ultimate intercession Jesus made for humanity on the cross with His precious blood once and for all.

- Readers will also learn God has consecrated all believers in Christ as intercessors, not just a select few as in the Old Testament, to stand in the gap for His mercy for those who even deserve His wrath and judgment.

- This book will help you understand how to maintain a close relationship with God and exhibit godly traits such as holiness, loving obedience to His word, and complete devotion to effective intercession. The Holy God has protocols and standards for His elected vessels, since none can approach Him with uncleanness. Jesus, the ultimate intercessor, satisfied all conditions to be the perfect High Priest. He obeyed all God's laws and communed daily with Him. So, God honored all His prayers.

- You will also learn Jesus' model for effective prayer, which includes worship, forgiveness, repentance, fasting, and perseverance before presenting our petitions and supplications, and how His model differs significantly from the Old Testament.

- Jesus warns us not to defile our body, which is the temple of the Holy Spirit, with evil such as adulteries, fornications, murders, thefts, covetousness, wickedness, deceit, lasciviousness, blasphemy, pride, and foolishness. They hinder our communion and have no place in the sight of God. Therefore, this book shares how intercessors can avoid and overcome such hindrances to effective intercession.

- The Bible clearly shows how Jesus led humanity's ultimate revival when He paid for our sins and reconciled our hearts with God. The goal was to perfect us like Himself and mandated believers to continue the ministry of intercession to save lost souls. This book teaches that

v

revival is God's initiative and predisposition alone and that any attempt without Jesus will fail. Thus, intercession brings revival and restores holiness, righteousness, joy, reconciliation, and a victorious life on earth to honor God.

Now that you have a glimpse of the book, continue onto the first chapter to learn about intercessory payers, which God initiated for the restoration of man. As you read this book, I encourage you to embrace the ministry of intercession that our Lord Jesus Christ has given us. God will truly bless you as you stand in the gap for others.

1

Intercessory Prayer

God initiated intercession for the restoration of humanity as our sins lead to misery and deterioration of the God-man relationship. *An intercessory prayer or intercession is a plea for God's mercy on behalf of others for restoration amid separation and misery.* It involves taking hold of God's promises in prayer until you see the desired change.

God foreknew of Adam and Eve's rebellion in the Garden of Eden, so He foreordained Jesus to stand in the gap for humanity before Creation. Before Jesus's earthly ministry, God consecrated godly prophets and priests with the privilege of accessing His presence to offer animal sacrifices for the atonement of sin and pray for His people. Many priests were faithful, others flouted God's laws and became ineffective.

> *"Wherefore he is able also to save them to the uttermost that come unto God by him, seeing he ever liveth to make intercession for them."* —**Hebrews 7:25**

At the appointed time, Jesus offered His sinless blood to atone for our sins. He pleaded for God's mercy for us and reconciled us with God through His death on the cross. Christians, now royal priests, have direct access to God to serve and offer spiritual sacrifices. Jesus has also given believers the ministry of reconciliation and intercession for the glory of God.

Why did God Initiate Intercession?

God is holy and hates sin. He established laws for humanity according to His righteousness and justified obedience to Him. When our hearts harden into sin and wander from God, it leads to punishment and separation from Him. As a merciful Father, He instituted intercession for our restoration when we drift from His presence and suffer the consequences of our sins. So God intends intercession to:

- Redeem man from rebellion and destruction;
- Release those who justly deserve God's judgment;
- Offer God's grace necessary for repentance and restoration;
- Set the captives and the oppressed free;
- Pave the way for man's redemption through Jesus;
- Benefit both the intercessor and the needy.

God created Adam and Eve in His image and likeness. He placed them in the lush and idyllic Garden of Eden, and established a covenant with them to be fruitful, multiply, and obey His sacred commandments (Genesis 1:26). He gave them dominion and established them as rulers over the earth's creatures and forbade them to eat from the tree of knowledge of good and evil amid the beautiful garden.

> *"And the Lord God commanded the man, saying, Of every tree of the garden thou mayest freely eat: But of the tree of the knowledge of good and evil, thou shalt not eat of it: for in the day that thou eatest thereof thou shalt surely die." — **Genesis 2:16-17***

The couple had daily fellowship with God. But Satan, through a serpent, enticed Eve to rebel against God's laws. Though God blessed the couple, she listened to deception and doubted God's goodness. She believed Satan's lies, ate the fruit from the tree of knowledge of good and evil, gave some to Adam, and broke the covenant.

2

God created Adam and Eve without corruption, but because of greed, they fell into temptation and sinned against God, bringing death to their souls, humanity, and the world. Thus, they lost innocence, purity, companionship, and authority. God expelled them from the garden, and their descendants and humanity inherited their corruption of sin. Since then, evil has enslaved humanity. Sin separates us from God and blinds us from our blessings (Isaiah 59:1-16). As the human population increased, so did evil and wickedness, but God sought faithful men to worship Him (Genesis 1-7).

Thus, God chose and ordained **priests and prophets** to stand in the gap *and* present supplications to the Lord for His people. He identified and established **covenants with godly people**, like Enoch. Yet, when men prospered, the cycle of disobedience continued. God saw how immense man's wickedness on earth was and how every plan devised by his mind was always nothing but evil. He regretted creating them.

However, God chose **Noah**, who was blameless and a righteous man. Noah found favor and walked with God. He asked Noah to build an ark to hold his wife, his three sons and their wives, and pairs of every animal. Then, God wiped out all but Noah and his family with a flood afterward and established a covenant with him. After Noah, man's disobedience continued. Some even attempted to build a tower called Babel to reach heaven. God saw their arrogance and so changed their language and scattered them.

Subsequently, God made a covenant with **Abraham** and his descendants, who became the nation of Israel. God promised to bless humanity through a descendant of Abraham. Jesus fulfilled this promise when He died and atoned for our sins and reconciled us to God.

3

Examples of intercessory prayers in the Old Testament

God anointed **prophets** and **priests** to intercede for His people in the Old Testament. These faithful people stood in the gap for God's mercies for others based on divine guidance. They usually offered animal sacrifices and offerings in their intercessions. For example:

Abraham's prayer for Sodom and Gomorrah

Abraham's intercession for the cities of Sodom and Gomorrah was the first intercessory prayer recorded in the Bible. God disclosed to Abraham His plans to destroy the vile cities for their rebellion when he extended hospitality to three traveling strangers, the Lord, and two angels in human form escorting Him.

> *"23And Abraham drew near, and said, Wilt thou also destroy the righteous with the wicked? 24Peradventure there be fifty righteous within the city: wilt thou also destroy and not spare the place for the fifty righteous that are therein? 25That be far from thee to do after this manner, to slay the righteous with the wicked: and that the righteous should be as the wicked, that be far from thee: Shall not the Judge of all the earth do right? 26And the Lord said, If I find in Sodom fifty righteous within the city, then I will spare all the place for their sakes. 27And Abraham answered and said, Behold now, I have taken upon me to speak unto the Lord, which am but dust and ashes: 28Peradventure there shall lack five of the fifty righteous: wilt thou destroy all the city for lack of five? And he said, If I find there forty and five, I will not destroy it. 29And he spake unto him yet again, and said, Peradventure there shall be forty found there. And he said I will not do it for forty's sake."* —
> ***Genesis 18:23-29***

Abraham's compassion for the cities of Sodom and Gomorrah reveals he cared for the righteous and disobedient. He wanted God to spare the righteous people who lived in Sodom (Amos 3:7-8).

> *"30And he said unto him, Oh let not the Lord be angry, and I will speak Peradventure there shall thirty be found there. And he said I will not do it if I find thirty there. 31And he said, Behold now, I have taken upon me to speak unto the Lord: Peradventure there shall be twenty found there. And he said, I will not destroy it for twenty's sake. 32And he said, Oh let not the Lord be angry, and I will speak yet, but this once: Peradventure ten shall be found there. And he said, I will not destroy it for ten's sake."* — **Genesis 18:31-32**

The iniquity of the cities wearied Lot and his family, but God offered to save them from His imminent wrath. He considered Abraham's persistence in seeking mercy to save the righteous from the impending calamity on the cities. Abraham respectfully acknowledged God's greatness and mercy in his covenant communion with Him. He humbly bargained with Him not to destroy Sodom if He found ten righteous people in the city.

God judges righteously according to our deeds, but His mercy delivers the underserved. He spared Lot and his two daughters and sent two angels to the city, who destroyed it when they could not find the ten required people. The destruction of the cities reminds us of the cost of rebellion against God. Sin has consequences, though God is loving and merciful. The cities indulged in sexual immorality and perversions. God takes pleasure in our bold but humble desire to intercede for other people. So, we do not have to reject opportunities but intercede for others in humility.

5

Abraham's intercession for Abimelech

Abraham traveled between Kadesh and Shur and stayed in Gerar. He made a terrible decision by presenting his wife, Sarah, as his sister to avoid attacks by the men of Gerar. When the king of Gerar, Abimelech, heard it, he brought Sarah to the palace and planned to keep her as his wife. Yet, God warned Abimelech that he had taken a prophet's wife in a dream. Abimelech pleaded for mercy because he had taken her in innocence, and God prevented him from touching Sarah.

> *"7 Now therefore restore the man his wife; for he is a prophet, and he shall pray for thee, and thou shalt live: and if thou restore her not, know thou that thou shalt surely die, thou, and all that are thine."* — **Genesis 20:7**

God asked Abraham to pray for Abimelech and his household when he restored Sarah to Abraham.

> *"17 So Abraham prayed unto God: and God healed Abimelech, and his wife, and his maidservants; and they bare children."* — **Genesis 20:17**

So, Abraham prayed, and God healed King Abimelech, his wife, and all the maidservants, reopening the womb of everyone in Abimelech's household, and they bore children (Genesis 20:1-18). Therefore, we must allow God to rule our hearts to avoid sin as we live for Him and pray for those who despise us and covet our blessings. God has warned us to not seek revenge or bear a grudge against anyone, but to love our neighbor as ourselves, for He is the Lord. Scriptures also say If your enemy is hungry, give him bread to eat, and if he is thirsty, give him water to drink, for you will heap burning coals on his head.

Job's Intercession for his friends

Job was a rich man who lived in Uz. He was blameless and upright before God. The Bible says that Job usually prayed for his children after they held feasts in their homes. He offered burnt sacrifices to atone for any wrongdoing by his children during these feasts.

God touted Job's righteousness, but Satan rebutted, saying that Job feared God only because He had blessed him with riches and protection. Satan further mentioned Job would curse God if He removed these blessings from him. Thus, God allowed Satan to torment Job, and he lost everything he had, including his children. But Job still blessed God despite his losses. Defeated, Satan sought God's permission to put sores on Job. Yet, despite his suffering, Job never doubted God's faithfulness, even when his wife said he should curse God and die.

Eliphaz, Bildad, and Zophar, Job's three friends, came to visit him, mourning in silence for seven days. Afterward, they argued with Job about the cause of his predicament. When Job insisted on his innocence, they falsely accused him of suffering from the consequences of his sins. As a result, Job became bitter and asked God to show him his sins if he had offended Him. Afterward, God intervened and questioned Job for his self-righteous attitude. Job beheld God's magnificence and realized his unworthiness. The Lord's revelation shattered Job's self-righteousness. He understood that his knowledge of God was imperfect and skewed. God humbled him, and he repented.

> *"I have heard of You by the hearing of the ear, but now my eye sees You. Therefore, I abhor myself, and repent in dust and ashes."—**Job 42:5-6***

7

Later, Job prayed for his friends as the Lord told him because the Lord refused to accept their prayers. As Job did, we need to **intercede for our friends**, even if they slander us. While suffering, Job prayed for his friends, and they received blessings that none of them deserved.

The Lord can transform the hearts of those who have wronged us if we will forgive and pray for them. Job's oppression and disappointment ended after the Lord accepted his intercession. God restored Job not because of his righteousness, but by the Lord's mercy.

> *"⁸ Therefore take unto you now seven bullocks and seven rams, and go to my servant Job, and offer up for yourselves a burnt offering; and my servant Job shall pray for you: for him will I accept: lest I deal with you after your folly, in that ye have not spoken of me the thing which is right, like my servant Job.⁹ So Eliphaz the Temanite and Bildad the Shuhite and Zophar the Naamathite went, and did according as the* LORD *commanded them: the* LORD *also accepted Job.¹⁰ And the* LORD *turned the captivity of Job, when he prayed for his friends: also the* LORD *gave Job twice as much as he had before." — **Job 42:8-10***

God graciously restored Job's blessings after Job interceded for his friends. God doubled Job's fortunes. So, it is necessary to pray for friends or foes even in times of challenges, and God will release us from whatever holds us in bondage.

Moses Intercedes for Israel

God chose **Moses as a leader, prophet, and intercessor** to take Israel from captivity in Egypt to Canaan. Moses was God's spokesperson for Israel during the exodus. He often pleaded for them to turn from their many sins to stop God's wrath. He interceded for God's mercy for Israel by reminding God of His promises to Abraham, Isaac, and Jacob. Thus, his many intercessions changed Israel's trajectory for good. He also received divine commands on priestly duties and built and furnished the tabernacle, a temporary place for worship. God's glory filled the Most Holy place of the sanctuary during the passage through the wilderness into the Promised Land.

Having left Egypt, the Israelites set up camp at Mount Sinai. There, Moses made a notable intercession at Mount Sinai when Israel forgot the Lord's goodness and indulged in idolatry. This terrible sin placed the entire nation in disastrous circumstances, as God wanted to destroy them. But Moses stepped in and pleaded for His mercy.

Moses had ascended the mountain of the Lord and spent 40 days and nights receiving the tablets of the Ten Commandments from God. Distressed by Moses' delay in returning to the camp, the Israelites coerced Aaron, Moses' brother, to fashion a golden calf. They worshiped the molten image since they did not know the fate of their leader and declared it their god, who delivered them from Egypt, and a helper to enter the Promised Land. Idol worship was an unforgivable abomination, for the people regarded the calf as their god, contrary to their promise to serve God alone (Exodus 17). Thus, God made Moses aware of Israel's idolatrous conduct at the foot of the mountain during the encounter. He also shared His intention and His judgment to wipe them out. When Moses descended from the mountain and saw their

9

evil deeds, he shattered the tablets of the law when he saw the people's unfaithfulness. After that, Moses made the Israelites drink the ground idol mold mixed with water. Finally, he slew 3,000 idolaters with the help of the devoted tribe of Levi. Then Moses stayed in the breach and pleaded with God in heart-rending supplications.

> *"11And Moses besought the LORD his God, and said, LORD, why doth thy wrath wax hot against thy people, brought forth out of the land of Egypt with great power, and with a mighty hand? 12 Wherefore should the Egyptians speak, and say, For mischief did he bring them out, to slay them in the mountains, and to consume them from the face of the earth? Turn from thy fierce wrath and repent of this evil against thy people. 13Remember Abraham, Isaac, and Israel, thy servants, to whom thou sparest by thine own self, and saidst unto them, I will multiply your seed as the stars of heaven, and all this land that I have spoken of will I give unto your seed, and they shall inherit it forever. 14And the Lord repented of the evil which he thought to do." — Exodus 32:11-14*

Moses' intimate fellowship with God endeared him as an effective intercessor. His love for his people, humility, and reverence for the Lord were apparent, as were his selflessness and devotion to the Lord. Moses' willingness to sacrifice himself and intercede for the rebellious and idolatrous Israel must inspire us to **pray for disobedient souls.**

His prayer appealed to God's mercy based upon His promises to Abraham, Isaac, and Jacob. By intervening, God spared the nation from destruction. Moses also showed servant leadership. We must intercede for people with God's word, even when they are unworthy.

10

Prayer for Miriam

Miriam was the daughter of Amram and Jochebed. She was Moses' older sister. When Jochebed, her mother, placed baby Moses in a basket on the Nile to escape death by the king of Egypt, she watched over her brother from afar. Pharaoh's daughter found the baby floating in the river and adopted him. Miriam led the Princess to Jochebed, who volunteered as a nanny.

Miriam played an essential role in the history of Israel and Moses. She led a celebration dance after the Israelites left Egypt and crossed the Red Sea. All the women followed Miriam, the prophetess, as she played the timbrel and danced after the Egyptians drowned in the Red Sea during the exodus from Egypt to the Promised Land.

Yet, during the journey through the wilderness, Mariam and Aaron queried Moses for marrying an Ethiopian. She also displeased God by questioning Moses' leadership over Israel. God called Moses, Aaron, and Miriam to meet Him at the Tent of Meeting in a pillar of clouds. God reprimanded Aaron and Miriam for speaking against His faithful servant, Moses (Numbers 12:7-8). Aaron and Miriam immediately realized their sins as God struck Miriam with leprosy.

Moses never sought revenge for their slander. Instead, he cared for his siblings and interceded for them. Therefore, God answered Moses' plea and healed Miriam after seven days. God hates disorder. That is why He commands us to submit to authority.

We must support our leaders in accomplishing the
shared objectives. Leaders must also be quick to forgive
and pray for those they lead.

Moses' prayer for Israel at Rephidim

After the Israelites left Egypt, the Amalekites were the first group that challenged and fought with Israel. When Israel camped in Rephidim, the Amalekites attacked Israel from behind and took old folks and children from the crowd during their journey. The Amalekites, descendants of Esau, were an ancient nomadic tribe described as Israel's enemy.

So Moses instructed Joshua to select men to battle the Amalekites. In battle, Moses, Aaron, and Hur went to the top of the hill. Israel won when Moses held up his hand, but Amalek prevailed when he let it down. Moses' hands became heavy, so he sat on a stone while Aaron and Hur supported his hands until the sun went down. In this manner, Joshua defeated Amalek with the sword (Exodus 17). Later, God told Moses to document the event as a memorial so the Israelites would not forget. He promised Amalek destruction because of their wickedness.

> *"So Joshua fought the Amalekites as Moses had ordered, and Moses, Aaron and Hur went to the top of the hill. As long as Moses held up his hands, the Israelites were winning, but whenever he lowered his hands, the Amalekites were winning. When Moses' hands grew tired, they took a stone and put it under him and he sat on it. Aaron and Hur held his hands up— one on one side, one on the other — so that his hands remained steady till sunset."* — **Exodus 17:11, 12**

After that, Moses built an altar at Rephidim and called it Jehovah Nissi. God taught Israel that He alone gives protection and victory.

We can only rise above our enemies and situations
when we depend on God.

Moses prays for Pharaoh

Israel had stayed in Egypt for four generations and increased in population and wealth and became a threat to the host. Fearing revolt, an envious Egyptian king steadily enslaved them. God sent Moses to free His people from slavery.

> *"Then the LORD said to Moses, Go to Pharaoh and say to him, This is what the LORD says: Let my people go, so that they may worship me. 2 If you refuse to let them go, I will plague your whole country with frogs. 3 The Nile will teem with frogs. They will come up into your palace and your bedroom and onto your bed, into the houses of your officials and on your people, and into your ovens and kneading troughs.4The frogs will go up on you and your people and all your officials." —- Exodus 6:1-5*

Nonetheless, Pharaoh did not heed God's intervention to let His people go until He hammered Egypt with a series of plagues. Pharaoh solicited Moses.

> *"Then Pharaoh summoned Moses and Aaron. This time I have sinned, he said to them. The Lord is in the right, and I and my people are in the wrong. 28 Pray to the Lord, for we have had enough thunder and hail. I will let you go; you don't have to stay any longer." — Exodus 12:31-32*

Moses intervened when He spread out his hands toward the LORD; the thunder and hail stopped, and the rain no longer poured down on the land. Besides, the frogs, rain, hail, thunder, locusts, and darkness to stop.

Intercession at the Wilderness of Paran

Moses sent out spies from each tribe of Israel to assess the land of Canaan. Two out of twelve spies returned with an excellent report. However, the rest discouraged the people with their evil accounts. They warned Israel could not take the land because the inhabitants were giants living in fortified cities. The Israelites raised their voices and wept bitterly in the tents when they heard the negative report of the ten spies.

So, in fury and confusion, they thought dying in Egypt was better than perishing in the wilderness at the hands of the inhabitants of Canaan. Upon hearing the Israelites' complaint about their desire to return to Egypt, Moses and Aaron fell to their knees in grief before the entire congregation of the Israelites. They lamented over Israel's lack of faith that God would fight and deliver them from their enemies and give them the promised land.

> *"And the Lord said to Moses, How long will these people despise me? And how long will they refuse to believe in me, despite all the signs that I have done among them? I will strike them with pestilence and disinherit them, and I will make of you a nation greater and mightier than they." — **Numbers 14:11-12***

However, because of Israel's rebellion at Kadesh Barnea, God wanted to strike them with pestilence, disinherit them, and make Moses a more significant and mightier nation than Israel (Numbers 14:2). God told Moses: "Now let me alone so that my wrath may burn hot against them, and I may consume them, and of you, I will make a great nation" (Exodus 32:10). Moses was not amused but interceded for the people.

He asked the Lord to forgive them for their rebellious attitude. He told God that the Egyptians would tell the people of Canaan that God had taken Israel out of Egypt with great power but could not bring the people to Canaan, so He killed them in the wilderness. Moses did not say that Israel's punishment was unjust. God did not disinherit the people in answer to Moses' prayer, but the generation of those who rebelled against God, except Joshua and Caleb, did not enter the Promised Land.

> *"17 And now, I beseech thee, let the power of my lord be great, according as thou hast spoken, saying, The LORD is longsuffering, and of great mercy, forgiving iniquity and transgression, and by no means clearing the guilty, visiting the iniquity of the fathers upon the children unto the third and fourth generation. 19 Pardon, I beseech thee, the iniquity of this people according unto the greatness of thy mercy, and as thou hast forgiven this people, from Egypt even until now. 20 And the LORD said, I have pardoned according to thy word:"*
> *— Number 14:17-20*

Furthermore, Moses' prayer on behalf of the rebellious Israel shows the power of prayer and how intercession can turn dire situations around.

We can obtain the grace and mercy of God
when we pray. God wants no one to perish
because of sin, so He ordains intercessors
to intercede.

Rebellion against Moses and intercession

Korah, Dathan, and Abiram, along with 250 conspirators, rebelled against Moses' and Aaron's leadership and priesthood. God punished them and their families. As a result, the people of Israel gathered against Moses and Aaron and blamed them for the deaths of Korah and his cohorts. God punished them with a plague, but Moses and Aaron interceded, and the plague stopped.

Besides those who died in Korah's affair, 14,700 died in the plague. Fear and envy caused a rebellion against Moses, but he interceded fervently according to the promises and glory of God. When the plague had started among the people, Aaron offered incense and atoned for them. As he stood between the living and the dead, the plague stopped.

Also, Israel grumbled against God and Moses because they had no water. They said Moses wished they had died when their brothers fell dead before the Lord. They wanted to know why Moses brought them from Egypt to the wilderness. Because of their complaints and unbelief, God sent venomous snakes among the people, and many of the Israelites died. The Israelites came to Moses and said, "We know we sinned when we spoke against the Lord and you. Pray to the Lord. Ask him to take away these snakes." So, Moses prayed for them. Aaron and Moses fell on their faces at the tent's entrance, and God appeared to them. He also prayed, and the plague of the fiery serpents ceased.

Later, God established a covenant with the Israelites and gave them laws to obey for blessings in the Promised Land. Difficult circumstances must not offend us to grumble or question the character of God, but to trust Him for victory.

Priesthood and intercession in Israel

The priesthood and intercessory duties officially began after God had delivered Israel from slavery in Egypt. They needed a mediator to atone for their sin. God chose and consecrated Aaron and his descendants from the tribe of Levi as priests to intercede for Israel.

> *"⁶ And unto Me you shall be a kingdom of priests and a holy nation. These are the words that you are to speak to the Israelites." — **Exodus 19:5,6***

Aaron was Moses' assistant. God also chose the Levites to serve at the Temple because they declared their allegiance to Him after Moses returned from Mount Sinai and saw Israel's abominations. Moses offered the Israelites the opportunity to make a stand and serve the Lord. The Levites sided with Moses and the Lord. Also, they were the only significant tribe that stood for God's cause after worshipping the golden calf idol incident. Thus, Aaron became the first High Priest and the ancestor of Israel.

> *"And take thou unto thee Aaron thy brother, and his sons with him, from among the children of Israel, that he may minister unto me in the priest's office, even Aaron, Nadab and Abihu, Eleazar and Ithamar, Aaron's sons." — **Exodus 28:1***

God allowed only the priests to minister before Him. He also directed the priests to learn and teach the law and approach Him with their prayer requests for Israel. The high priest atoned for the people's sins before the Mercy Seat yearly with a sprinkling of animal blood. But, when the later priests failed in this noble mandate, God honored those who obeyed His laws. He continued to use faithful priests, but He chose prophets and godly leaders to intercede for Israel.

Samuel's prayer for Israel

God chose and consecrated **Samuel** as **a prophet and judge** in Israel. Samuel was born to Elkanah and Hannah after a promise his barren mother made to God during prayers (1 Samuel 1). After birth, his parents dedicated him as a child to the Lord to redeem the promise. Eli, the high priest, raised him. God favored the obedient Samuel, who served as a judge and a prophet during the reign of Saul.

Eli had problems with his two sons, Phinehas and Hophni, who coveted most of the meat from sacrifices and committed adultery with the women who served at the sanctuary entrance. Covetousness and adultery brought the worship of God into disrepute. Eli did nothing beyond verbally rebuking his sons when God warned him through revelations, aside from the costs of failing to repent concerning his sons. God hates sin, and He judges sinners who do not repent. Thus, He punished Eli and his sons. Later, God ordained Samuel as a prophet and the judge of Israel after Eli died.

Samuel placed God first in his life. He obediently and faithfully served God and Israel. He had an elevated level of integrity. Samuel led Israel to repent from idolatry, and the Lord God responded to their cry. As a prophet and a great man of prayer, he interceded for Israel. Israel was not faithful to God at one point. But when they repented and turned from following idols, the Lord God responded to their cry.

> *"³ And Samuel spake unto all the house of Israel, saying, If ye do return unto the LORD with all your hearts, then put away the strange gods and Ashtaroth from among you, and prepare your hearts unto the LORD, and serve him only: and he will deliver you out of the hand of the Philistines. — **1 Samuel 7:3***

Samuel prayed for Israel during the war that defeated the Philistines. He offered burnt sacrifices to the Lord on behalf of the Israelites (1 Samuel 7:7-8). He cried out, asking the Lord to deliver the Israelites. God answered while Samuel offered the sacrifice to Him. As the Philistine warriors arrived, the Israelites were unprepared for battle; that day, the Lord struck the Philistines with great thunder, discomfiting and defeating them.

> *"⁴ Then the children of Israel did put away Baalim and Ashtaroth and served the LORD only. ⁵ And Samuel said, Gather all Israel to Mizpeh, and I will pray for you unto the LORD. ⁶ And they gathered together to Mizpeh, and drew water, and poured it out before the LORD, and fasted on that day, and said there, We have sinned against the LORD. And Samuel judged the children of Israel in Mizpeh."* — *1 Samuel 7:4-6*

The army of Israel pursued the Philistines and smote them. Thus, the Philistine domination over Israel ended with all captured cities restored to Israel. No nation invaded Israel all the days of Samuel, for the LORD was with him. The Israelites and the Amorites also had peace. Samuel stood in the gap and helped Israel's army fight against the Philistines and other enemy nations that tried to invade Israel.

During the drought and famine when the people had disobeyed in Israel, Samuel prayed, and God sent thunder and rain. So all the people stood in awe of the Lord and of Samuel. He advised Israel to repent from serving unprofitable idols and serve God with all their hearts. He promised to intercede for Israel and teach them the ways of God. He also warned the people not to persist in doing evil, so both they and their king will perish.

David's Intercession for Israel

David was a shepherd boy who became the second king of ancient Israel after the demise of King Saul. He was an intercessor and worshipper of God. Once, King David took a census, which was contrary to God's words. Then, David said to the Lord: "I have sinned greatly against you." He asked God to forgive him and take away his guilt. God gave David the choice between three punishments to be carried out against him: three years of famine for his land, three months of running from his enemies as they pursued him, and a plague that would last for three days. David pleaded with God to let him fall under His hands. However, he sent a plague to Israel that very morning, which led to the death of 70,000 people.

> *"No," replied the king, "I insist on paying a price, for I will not offer to the LORD my God burnt offerings that cost me nothing." So David bought the threshing floor and the oxen for fifty shekels of silver. 25And there he built an altar to the LORD and offered burnt offerings and peace offerings. Then the LORD answered the prayers on behalf of the land, and the plague upon Israel was halted. — **2 Samuel 24:25***

On the same day, God instructed David to build an altar on the floor of the threshing barn owned by Jebusites and Arunah's. David then went to Araunah and told him he wanted to purchase his threshing floor so that he could build an altar for God so the plague would end. Araunah finally offered it, along with some oxen, to David for free, but David refused. Therefore, David paid Araunah with silver. The king also built an altar for the Lord and sacrificed burnt offerings and fellowship offerings on it. As a result, God answered his prayer, and the plague ended (2 Samuel 24).

20

Solomon's Intercession for Israel

Solomon was the third and final monarch of united Israel after Saul and David, his father. He built the magnificent temple in Jerusalem and invited the leaders of Israel for dedication, fulfilling God's promise to David. During the dedication, a sense of solemnity and reverence filled the atmosphere. The priests brought the ark of the covenant to the Sanctuary in the Most Holy Place of the temple. They took it from the tent where David had placed it. The Ark contained the tablets of the Ten Commandments from Mount Sinai. The glory of the Lord filled the Holy Place after the animal sacrifice and priestly songs. Then Solomon blessed Israel, reminding them he was carrying out his father David's promise to God. He prayed for further fulfillment of God's promises and ask God to show mercy to Israel when they go astray. He pleaded for Israel's victory in battle.

> *"⁴⁴ If thy people go out to battle against their enemy, whithersoever thou shalt send them, and shall pray unto the LORD toward the city which thou hast chosen, and toward the house that I have built for thy name:⁴⁵ Then hear thou in heaven their prayer and their supplication, and maintain their cause.⁶ If they sin against thee, (for there is no man that sinneth not,) and thou be angry with — them, and deliver them to the enemy, so that they carry them away captives unto the land of the enemy, far or near;⁴⁷ Yet if they shall bethink themselves in the land whither they were carried captives, and repent, and make supplication unto thee in the land of them that carried them captives, saying, We have sinned, and have done perversely, we have committed wickedness." — 1 Kings 8:44-47*

Solomon also asked that the Lord may forgive and restore Israel from captivity and suffering when they repent. Besides, he prayed that God may hear the prayers of strangers who come from afar to pray toward the Temple, that all people may know God's name.

> *"[41]Moreover concerning a stranger, that is not of thy people Israel, but cometh out of a far country for thy name's sake; [42](For they shall hear of thy great name, and of thy strong hand, and of thy stretched out arm;) when he shall come and pray toward this house; [43]Hear thou in heaven thy dwelling place, and do according to all that the stranger calleth to thee for: that all people of the earth may know thy name, to fear thee, as do thy people Israel; and that they may know that this house, which I have builded, is called by thy name." — 1* **Kings 8:41-43**

When Solomon had finished, the LORD appeared to him a second time, as he had appeared to him at Gibeon. and said to him, "I have heard the prayer and plea you have made before me, I have consecrated this temple, which you have built, by putting my Name there forever. My eyes and my heart will always be there. [4]As for you, if you walk before me faithfully with integrity of heart and uprightness, as David your father did, and do all I command and observe my decrees and laws, [5] I will establish your royal throne over Israel forever, as I promised David your father when I said, 'You shall never cease to have a successor on the throne of Israel." He warned against disobedience (1 Kings 9:2-9). We pray that the LORD, our God, will protect us and be with us always, just as he did for our ancestors. May he open our hearts to him, so that we will walk in obedience to him and uphold his decrees, rules, and mandates.

Prophet Elijah

Elijah was a Hebrew prophet. He lived in the Northern kingdom of Israel during the twenty-two-year reign of Ahab. Ahab and his wife Jezebel led Israel to worship idols and murdered God's prophets. However, Elijah challenged the people for the corruption and defilement of worshipping Baal, contrary to God's laws.

> *"36Elijah the prophet came near, and said, LORD God of Abraham, Isaac, and of Israel, let it be known this day that thou art God in Israel, and that I am thy servant, and that I have done all these things at thy word.37 Hear me, O LORD, hear me, that this people may know that thou art the LORD God, and that thou hast turned their heart back again.38 Then the fire of the LORD fell and consumed the burnt sacrifice, and the wood, and the stones, and the dust, and licked up the water that was in the trench. 39 And when all the people saw it, they fell on their faces: and they said, The LORD, he is the God; the LORD, he is the God. — 1 Kings 18:36-39*

Elijah contested the prophets of Baal when He asked God to reveal Himself to the people by fire. The prophets of Baal prayed in vain, as Baal could not consume their sacrifice without fire. But God answered Elijah by fire, and the people repented and turned to God.

> *"O Lord, God of Abraham, Isaac, and Israel, let it be known this day that you are God in Israel, and that I am your servant, and that I have done all these things at your word. Answer me, O Lord, answer me, that these people may know that you, O Lord, are God and that you have turned their hearts back."*
> *— 1 Kings 18:36-37*

23

Nehemiah's Prayer, Identifying with the Sins of His People

Nehemiah was a Jewish leader who oversaw the restoration of the broken walls of Jerusalem with the help of the Babylonian King Artaxerxes, whom he served. When he heard about Jerusalem's broken-down walls, he prayed to the Lord for the opportunity to return and rebuild the walls. He went with a heart of confession and repentance before God. Nehemiah humbly fasted, prayed, and reminded God of their commitment to obedience from the time of Moses. He confessed Israel's and his sins of corruption and failures against God to keep the laws given to Moses. Moreover, Nehemiah acknowledged that their disobedience had led to their exile in Babylon. Therefore, he asked for mercy and urged God to fulfill His promise to restore the people.

> *"5 And said, I beseech thee, O LORD God of heaven, the great and terrible God, that keepeth covenant and mercy for them that love him and observe his commandments: ⁶Let thine ear now be attentive, and thine eyes open, that thou mayest hear the prayer of thy servant, which I pray before thee now, day and night, for the children of Israel thy servants, and confess the sins of the children of Israel, which we have sinned against thee: both I and my father's house have sinned. 7 We have dealt very corruptly against thee, and have not kept the laws, nor the statutes, nor the judgments, which thou commandedst thy servant Moses." — Nehemiah 1:5-7*

God favored Nehemiah before the King, who assisted him in returning and rebuilding the walls of Jerusalem. Later, Nehemiah brokered peace among Judah over Persian taxes. He used prayer, praise, persistence, and faith in God to revive Judah and restore God's plan.

Ezra intercedes for Israel

Ezra was a priest, scribe, and descendant of Aaron. For the zeal for God and His Law, he led a group of Jews back to Israel during King Artaxerxes' reign over the Persian Empire. When Ezra saw the rebuilding of the Temple and the unity of the tribes, he interceded for Judah. He also publicly stood in the gap and read the word of God to Israel. As a result, they repented and worshiped God thirteen years after Nehemiah restored the shattered walls. Afterward, they appealed to God for mercy by reckoning their sins and pledging to serve God wholeheartedly.

> *"5And at the evening sacrifice, I arose up from my heaviness; and having rent my garment and my mantle, I fell upon my knees, and spread out my hands unto the LORD my God, 6And said, O my God, I am ashamed and blush to lift my face to thee, my God: for our iniquities are increased over our head, and our trespass is grown up unto the heavens. 7Since the days of our fathers have we been in a great trespass unto this day; and for our iniquities have we, our kings, and our priests, been delivered into the hand of the kings of the lands, to the sword, to captivity, and to spoil, and the confusion of face, as it is this day." — Ezra 9:5-7*

Next, Ezra led his group to affirm an existing agreement. This meant stopping intermarriage with non-Jews, trading on the Sabbath, observing the land fallow, and debt erasure in the seventh year. Also, they maintained the Temple and its services and staffed the Temple with priests and Levites settled by a lot. Furthermore, they provided needs of the Temple, such as wood and the first fruits for priests. Last, they redeemed firstborn sons and sacrificed those of livestock.

Queen Esther's intercession for the Jews

Esther was an orphan adopted by her uncle, Mordecai. While in exile in Shushan, Mordecai became her mentor and confidant. She later became the beautiful Jewish wife of King Ahasuerus of Persia. Mordecai foiled a plot by two attendants to assassinate the king. Later, the king promoted Haman the Agagite, his servant, to the greatest position in the court, and all royal officials at the king's gate kneeled and honored Haman, as the king had ordered. But Mordecai would not kneel or pay him tribute.

Therefore, Haman felt indignant toward Mordecai for his perceived lack of respect. He sought revenge for his humiliation by casting lots to select the day and time to kill all the Jews. Haman later influenced the King to make an order for the execution of Jews throughout the provinces because they did not obey the king's laws. Faced with the destruction in Haman's hands, Mordecai consulted Esther. Esther realized it was not in her power to save the Jews. Therefore, she gathered the Jews and resorted to prayers and fasting.

> *"Then answered Esther, and said, My petition and my request is If I have found favor in the sight of the king, and if it pleases the king to grant my petition and to perform my request, let the king and Haman come to the banquet that I shall prepare for them, and I will do tomorrow as the king hath said."* —
> ***Esther 5:8***

After the fast, Esther made her case about the plot of the extinction of her people before the king. Enraged by the plot, the king got Haman impaled on the pole he had set up for Mordecai. So, God places us to intercede on His glory in challenging situations. Besides, if you do not act for the Lord, someone else will.

Daniel's Prayer, Identifying with the sins of Judah

Daniel was a prince of Judah. He was a righteous man from the ancestry of David in Israel. He was one of the captured nobles exiled to Babylon by King Nebuchadnezzar. He lived an exceptionally long life and saw the fall of Assyria by the Medes and Persians. Daniel interceded for the Jewish people to return to God. While Daniel was in Babylonian captivity, he read Jeremiah's prophecy that the exile would last 70 years. Thus, he set his heart toward God with fasting, sackcloth, and ashes when he realized that the 70 years had almost ended.

> *"⁴O Lord, the great and dreadful God, keeping the covenant and mercy to them that love him, and to them that keep his commandments;⁵ We have sinned, and have committed iniquity, and have done wickedly, and have rebelled, even by departing from thy precepts and from thy judgments: ⁶ Neither have we hearkened unto thy servants the prophets, which spake in thy name to our kings, our princes, and our fathers, and to all the people of the land. ⁷ O LORD, righteousness belongeth unto thee, but unto us confusion of faces, as at this day; to the men of Judah, and to the inhabitants of Jerusalem, and unto all Israel, that are near, and that are far off, through all the countries whither thou hast driven them, because of their trespass that they have trespassed against thee." —*
> *Daniel 9:4-7*

Daniel prayed, reminding God of His faithfulness. He acknowledged they deserved His punishment. Yet Daniel pleaded for God's mercy to restore Israel to their homeland. The premise for all answered prayers is His name and promises (Daniel 9:17-19). So, God answered Daniel and gave him more revelations about future events.

Intercession in the New Testament

The New Testament brought in a new covenant between God and humanity, sealed by the blood of Jesus. Unlike the Old Testament, where the priests made intercession through daily and seasonal animal sacrifices and offerings, Jesus paid for our sins with His blood on the cross once and for all.

This ultimate intercession has given every Christian access to God's presence because Jesus has reconciled us to God and made us priests of the Lord. Therefore, God does not require animal sacrifice for intercession; and not only a selected few may intercede. Before Jesus, God sent John the Baptist to prepare the people's hearts for the new covenant.

The Ministry of John the Baptist

John was a Jewish prophet. The father, Zechariah, was a priest who belonged to the priestly division of Abijah; in the time of Herod, king of Judea. The mother, Elizabeth, was also a descendant of Aaron. He was a messenger, and the forerunner of Jesus sent to prepare the way for the coming of the promised Messiah.

Isaiah and Malachi foretold His birth "I will send my messenger ahead of you, who will prepare your way a voice of one calling in the wilderness, 'Prepare the way for the Lord, make straight paths for him (Isaiah 40:3)

John grew and became strong in spirit, and he lived and spent lots of time praying in the wilderness until he appeared publicly in Israel. John preached the doctrine of repentance for the remission of sins. He also immersed the people in the water as a symbol of repentance.

Seeing many people coming to his baptism, he admonished them to bear worthy fruits of repentance.

> *"⁷ Then said he to the multitude that came forth to be baptized of him, O generation of vipers, who hath warned you to flee from the wrath to come? ⁸Bring forth, therefore, fruits worthy of repentance, and begin not to say within yourselves, We have Abraham to our father: for I say unto you, That God is able of these stones to raise up children unto Abraham. ⁹ And now also the axe is laid unto the root of the trees: every tree therefore which bringeth not forth good fruit is hewn down and cast into the fire."* — **Luke 3:7-8**

Different groups of people, such as tax collectors, soldiers, and others, asked what they should do:

> *"¹² Then came also publicans to be baptized, and said unto him, Master, what shall we do?¹³ And he said unto them, Exact no more than that which is appointed you.¹⁴ And the soldiers likewise demanded of him, saying, And what shall we do? And he said unto them, Do violence to no man, neither accuse any falsely; and be content with your wages."* — **Luke 3:11- 14**

The people revered him as a prophet. He led Israel to repent of their sins and baptized the Messiah.

The Ultimate Intercession

When Jesus Christ died for us, He reconciled us to God (1 Peter 3:19; Colossians 1:20). Jesus is the **ultimate intercessor** who lives forever as the mediator, representing humanity before the throne of God. He **bridged the gap** between humanity and God through redemption by

His sacrifices on the cross. The blood sacrifice under the Law could not save the people, but the precious **blood of Jesus saved us from our sins**.

Jesus brought grace and truth. For instance,

- He taught us the true nature of God and how to worship Him.
- He showed mercy to all who came to Him for help, including the woman caught in adultery by the stone-wielding Pharisees, though she deserved to die under the Law. Moreover, He healed and restored lepers, the blind, and a variety of other sick people with compassion when they sought him.
- Also, Jesus forgave sinners so that God would heal them.
- He healed Peter's mother-in-law, the man with the shriveled hand; the forty-year-old man who was born blind. He raised people from the dead, including Lazarus and the widow's son. While with the disciples, Jesus prayed for Peter's repentance before Satan tempted him to deny Him. Jesus had chosen Peter to lead the Church after his departure, but Satan planned to seduce and rob him of his ministry.

   *"Simon, Simon, behold, Satan has desired to have you, that he may sift you as wheat: But I have prayed for thee, that thy faith fails not: and when thou art converted, strengthen thy brethren." — **Luke 22:31-33***

Further, Jesus' prayer for His disciples contains three essential elements. **First,** God had chosen them, so they belonged to Him. **Second,** He asked them to be united as He united with the Father. **The third** is the petition for the protection of the twelve disciples and all who would believe in Him.

> *"Neither pray I for these alone, but for them also which shall believe on me through their word; [21] That they all may be one; as thou, Father, art in me, and I in thee, that they also may be one in us: that the world may believe that thou hast sent me.[22] And the glory which thou gavest me I have given them; that they may be one, even as we are one:[23] I in them, and thou in me, that they may be made perfect in one; and that the world may know that thou hast sent me, and hast loved them, as thou hast loved me.[24] Father, I will that they also, whom thou hast given me, be with me where I am; that they may behold my glory, which thou hast given me: for thou lovedst me before the foundation of the world. O righteous Father, the world hath not known thee: but I have known thee, and these have known that thou hast sent me." — John 17:20-25*

He prayed for His crucifiers and adversaries during His perfect life and atoning sacrifice on the cross. He interceded for His disciples and believers. Even after his ascension, he continues to do so. Jesus now sits at the right hand of God, interceding for us.

Jesus is a high priest who can sympathize with our weaknesses. Though the people tempted him, he never sinned (Matthew 4:1-10). He saves because of His goodness. He justifies and sanctifies believers. When we give our lives to Jesus, He identifies with us. He transforms us into His image by His grace. The Lord defends and vindicates us against the accusations of Satan.

The Holy Spirit and Intercession

After His resurrection, Jesus told His disciples to remain in Jerusalem until they received the empowerment of the Holy Spirit to continue the ministry. He made a promise to His disciples that He would bring a "Helper" who would empower and teach them. So, on the day of Pentecost, a thanksgiving feast for the first fruits of the wheat harvest, as they gathered in an upper room to pray, they received the Holy Spirit and spoke in other tongues.

It amazed the people, but Peter explained it was the gift of the Spirit so that people could hear God's Word. After Peter preached to them, the Holy Spirit convicted them of their sins. They asked what they should do to be saved. Peter told them to repent of their sins and be baptized in the name of Jesus Christ for forgiveness.

About 3,000 people, who received Peter's sermon, got converted and baptized. In Jesus Christ, the Holy Spirit again bear every Christian. We are born of the Spirit, and the Holy Spirit seals our salvation (Ephesians 4:30).

> *"But you will receive power when the Holy Spirit comes on you, and you will be my witnesses in Jerusalem, in Judaea and Samaria, and to the end of the earth." — **Acts 1:8***

> *"I will ask the Father, and he will give you another Counselor to be with you forever - the Spirit of truth. The world cannot accept him because it neither sees him nor knows him. But you know him, for he lives with you and will be in you." — **John 14:16-18***

Prayer is *the avenue for developing a personal relationship with God to advance His kingdom.* Thus, He gave us the Holy Spirit, who enables us to obey His Word and leads us in prayer while walking in the Spirit. We are born of the Spirit, and the Holy Spirit seals our salvation. As we obey the word of God, we bear the fruit of the Spirit that pleases God.

> *"But the fruit of the Spirit is love, joy, peace, patience, kindness, goodness, faithfulness, gentleness, self-control; against such things, there is no law."* — **Galatians 5:22-23**

Also, God gives believers gifts for His purpose in the body of Christ. Only the Holy Spirit empowers us to optimize the use of the gifts for God's service. For instance, the disciples spoke in another tongue when the Holy Spirit came upon them at Pentecost. Those who speak in other languages with the power of the Holy Spirit display God's supernatural sign that they have been filled with the Holy Spirit. When we pray in tongues, we speak mysteries in the Spirit, and only God understands (1 Corinthians 14:2).

> *"⁴Now there are diversities of gifts, but the same Spirit. ⁵ And there are differences of administrations, but the same Lord. ⁶ And there are diversities of operations, but it is the same God which worketh all in all. ⁷ But the manifestation of the Spirit is given to every man to profit withal. ⁸For to one is given by the Spirit the word of wisdom; to another the word of knowledge by the same Spirit; ⁹To another faith by the same Spirit; to another the gifts of healing by the same Spirit; ¹⁰To another the working of miracles; to another prophecy; to another discerning of spirits; to another divers kinds of tongues; to another the interpretation of tongues."* — *1 Corinthians. 12:4-11*

The Holy Spirit also intercedes for us, especially when we do not know how to pray. Thus, the Holy Spirit takes responsibility since He knows our burdens, God's will, and what is best. The Holy Spirit helps us in our weaknesses when we feel overawed and do not know how we should pray to God. The Holy Spirit takes control when we have no words to communicate our requests in our most difficult hours.

> *"[26]Likewise the Spirit also helpeth our infirmities: for we know not what we should pray for as we ought: but the Spirit itself maketh intercession for us with groanings which cannot be uttered.[27]And he that searcheth the hearts knoweth what is the mind of the Spirit because he maketh intercession for the saints according to the will of God.[28] And we know that all things work together for good to them that love God, to them who are the called according to his purpose." — **Romans 8:26-28**

As Christians, **our primary mission** *is to witness the gospel through our words and deeds.*

We must reflect Jesus' character in our lives, not just in words. **The only viable way** is if the Holy Spirit moves through us. Through us, God continues to work miracles. We cannot do this without the help of the Holy Spirit.

The Holy Spirit intervenes and brings deliverance when problems are overwhelming. He works to bring us victory.

He intercedes for us and helps us pray with the will of God. But human words cannot express the intercession of the Spirit.

The Church prays for Peter

After Jesus' ascension, the church faced persecution. First, King Herod killed James and jailed Peter for preaching the Gospel. While Peter was in prison, the church earnestly prayed to God for him. Herod had planned to eliminate the leaders of the church and persecute the believers. Four squads of soldiers guarded Peter whilst he slept bound with two chains.

On the eve of his trial and execution, suddenly, an angel appeared, telling him to put on his clothes. He followed the angel out of the prison. On the way out, they passed two guard posts, and as they approached the prison gate, it opened on its own accord until Peter got to the city streets of Jerusalem, and the angel left him. He thought it was a dream until he realized it was real. God intervened and saved him. He stopped the plans of Herod and the Sanhedrin (Acts 12:3-19).

Thus, this example shows that **miracles occur when people collaboratively pray with sincerity**. Besides, corporate prayers played a vital role in the early Christian church.

> *"Again, I say unto you, that if two of you shall agree on earth as touching, ask, it shall be done for them of my Father which is in Heaven. That his name will be glorified." — **Matthew 18:19***

We stand to benefit when our hearts unite in prayer. So, we must not stop learning and growing in intercession. Indeed, gathering with other believers in fellowship and worship leads to growth in Him. There is power in a united intercession. Hence, praying with unity increases our authority and yields many results.

Epaphras' intercession for the Church

Epaphras became a faithful servant and a member of the church in Colosse. He was a man of prayer who persevered in long hours of prayer for the church. He willingly labored on his knees for the Colossian believers to stand and mature spiritually. Later, he visited Paul in Rome and brought a favorable report to Paul. The information encouraged Paul, who later sent him back to Colosse, bearing Paul's letter to the saints in that city. Paul commended Epaphras for his labor of love in the Lord's vineyard. Let us desire the spirit of intercession to pray for others consistently (Colossians 1:7-8; 4:2-13).

Paul Exhorts the Church to Intercede

Paul initially was an enemy of the Christian faith, but later became a fervent gospel preacher after Jesus Christ chose him. He founded several churches as he traveled around preaching the gospel in Asia Minor and Europe with the message of salvation to the Gentiles. Also, Paul called on believers to intercede for all men, including those in authority, to live in peace (Gal. 4:19; 1 Timothy 2:1-5).

In Conclusion

Intercessory prayer is a petition to God for His mercy to restore others. God initiated intercession to restore the God-man relationship, eroded by sin since the fall. Besides, He determines the conditions for intercessory prayers. He anointed the priests to stand in the gap for His people. However, some priests disobeyed God. Therefore, God chastised them and honored those who obeyed His word.

At the appointed time, Jesus manifested and interceded by atoning for our sins on the cross and reconciling us to God. He has made every believer a priest. Therefore, the Holy Spirit empowers intercessors to

36

approach God for others. It is a command for all men to pray without ceasing in the Spirit on all occasions. This contrasts with the Old Testament, where only the anointed few had the mandate to pray to God. Hence, the practice of intercession is still relevant to the body of Christ in contemporary Christian society. God restores faith in Him in challenging times when we intercede. It grieves God when we neglect to pray for others.

Intercession is a channel through which God releases blessings. God destroys the enemy's plan when we intercede. Thus, many intercessors prayed to God for the sake of people in history. The Prophets, Priests, Jesus, the ultimate intercessor, the Apostles, the early believers, and the church made intercessions. Therefore, all believers must stand in the gap for others.

The next chapter discusses intercessors and how Christ Jesus paid the sacrificial price to become the ultimate intercessor for humanity in the New Testament.

2

Intercessors

Are you saddened by the chaos and suffering in the world because of sin and the resultant separation from God? Then you share in God's desire and call for intercession in every aspect of our lives.

*Intercessors are God's **consecrated people** who pray for His mercy on others' behalf for restoration.*

Sin and death entered the world after Adam sinned. But God foreordained Jesus as our ultimate intercessor to redeem us. Before Jesus came, God sought and consecrated godly people, patriarchs, priests, and prophets, judges, and deliverers, as intercessors who prayed for His people in the Old Testament. Some of these intercessors were faithful to their mandate, while others failed because of disobedience. But God had promised a new covenant with the perfect High Priest. Isaiah, like many other prophets, prophesied about the Messiah when he said:

"The Spirit of the Lord God is upon me; because the Lord hath anointed me to preach good tidings unto the meek; he hath sent me to bind up the brokenhearted, to proclaim liberty to the captives, and the opening of the prison to them that are bound; To proclaim the acceptable year of the Lord, and the day of vengeance of our God; to comfort all that mourn;" — *Isa. 61:1-2*

Therefore, God anointed Jesus Christ the Great High Priest and the perfect intercessor who paid the ultimate sacrificial price to redeem humanity. Jesus has made Christians a royal priesthood to God to offer spiritual sacrifices acceptable through Him. He has mandated believers as intercessors to preach the Word and intercede for others in the Holy Spirit's ability for God's glory.

> *Let a man so account of us, as of the ministers of Christ, and stewards of the mysteries of God.[2] Moreover it is required in stewards, that a man be found faithful.[3] But with me it is a very small thing that I should be judged of you, or of man's judgment: yea, I judge not mine own self. —1 **Corinthians 4:1-3***

Apostle Peter also confirmed to the early believers scattered abroad that:

- Jesus had made them royal priests of God after obtaining mercy, though they were not originally part of His chosen people, Israel.
- Also Peter described the new priestly generation who will proclaim God's sacrifice in the form of praise among the nations.

> *"[9]But ye are a chosen generation, a royal priesthood, a holy nation, a peculiar people; that ye should shew forth the praises of him who hath called you out of darkness into his marvelous light: [10]Which in time past were not a people, but are now the people of God: which had not obtained mercy, but now have obtained mercy." — 1 Peter 2:9-10*

Notable Intercessors in the Old Testament

Abraham

God told Abram to depart from his father's house for a land He would show him (Genesis 12:1). He promised to bless Abram with offspring and make him a great nation. Abram took his wife, Sarai, his nephew Lot, and left his father's house for Canaan. God had a covenant of circumcision with Abram and his descendants and changed his name to Abraham and renamed Sarai Sarah. Abraham had remarkable faith in God, and He blessed him abundantly with wealth, flocks, and camels (Genesis 17).

God eventually blessed Abraham with the covenant son, Isaac, at an old age. However, Abraham promptly obeyed God and prepared to sacrifice Isaac when God tested and commanded him to sacrifice him. He believed God could raise him. But God provided him with a sacrificial lamb in Isaac's stead. Thus, God counted this act of faith as righteousness and reaffirmed His covenant blessings to him (Genesis 22).

Abraham became the first recorded intercessor in the Bible when he interceded for Sodom. He pleaded for the redemption of Sodom when God divulged to him His decision to destroy the city for their sins. He endeared himself to God with the great faith that made him unique. Abraham was bold when he came to know that certain kings had captured Lot, his nephew, while he sojourned at Sodom. He and his men chased the captors, defeated them, and brought back Lot and all his possessions and people. Abraham was not selfish but gave Lot the choice of the portion of land to settle in before him. He ventured to face a powerful enemy to rescue Lot; moreover, he had a strong relationship with God. As a man who obeyed the commands of God and walked closely with Him, God revealed to him the imminent destruction of Sodom and Gomorrah. Abraham boldly stood in the gap as an intercessor and pleaded earnestly with God for Sodom and Gomorrah. He had an absolute conviction that God was a righteous judge and would save the righteous. Also, he built altars for God, gave Him the glory and praise, and depended on Him. He was also very hospitable to strangers.

> *"Shall I hide from Abraham what I am about to do seeing that Abraham shall surely become a great and mighty nation?"* — **Genesis 18:17-18**

The Bible described him as a friend of God because he was obedient (Genesis 18). God chose Abraham as the man through whom He would fulfill the promise of redemption for the world. He knew Abraham would bring up his children in the LORD's way. Thus, God made a covenant with him to give the land of Canaan to his descendants and bless the nations through him. Indeed, the Israelites later became enslaved people in Egypt and afterward entered Canaan.

Abraham still made mistakes. He wavered, listened to his wife's advice, and had a son with Hagar, the maid. Thus, he failed when he had a child with his maid. But God forgave him and warned him to walk faithfully before Him. So, he redeemed Abraham and Sarah, irrespective of their pitfalls. He also lied about Sarah to Abimelech out of fear for his life. Abraham led a righteous lifestyle. He lived to please God, which attracted God's blessings. He believed in God's plan without knowing what was ahead. God also fulfilled His promises to Abraham. Like Abraham, we must show compassion and love for others. So, we must have faith in God, stay close to Him, and intercede for others as God leads us.

The Prophet Moses

Amram and Jochebed gave birth to Moses in Egypt. Pharaoh's daughter rescued Moses from the water and raised him as her son when Jochebed hid him from Pharaoh's murderous decree. Moses fled Egypt to Midian after he murdered an Egyptian in defense of an Israelite and worked as a shepherd for his father-in-law, Jethro. After forty years, God spoke to Moses in a burning bush and asked him to return to Egypt to deliver His people from slavery. God tasked him to lead the Israelites out of Egypt to the Promised Land.

> *"And the Lord said, I have surely seen the affliction of my people which are in Egypt, and have heard their cry by reason of their taskmasters; for I know their sorrows; And I am come down to deliver them out of the hand of the Egyptians, and to bring them up out of that land unto a good land and a large, unto a land flowing with milk and honey; unto the place of the Canaanites, and the Hittites, and the Amorites, and the Perizzites, and the Hivite, and the Jebusites." — Exo. 3:7-8*

Moses obeyed God and became a mighty intercessor, prophet, and ruler for the Israelites. He stood in the gap and pleaded for God's mercy for the frequently disobedient Israelites during their forty-year journey to Canaan. He received commandments from God on behalf of the Israelites. Moses obeyed God's laws and orders in the face of vast challenges. He had great faith in God, even when others doubted him. He had holy boldness and risked his own life for Israel.

Besides, God did tremendous miracles through him. Moses led the Israelites out of Egypt, and they crossed the Red Sea on foot. God gave the law through him. He was not selfish because he rejected God's promise to choose him and destroy the Israelites for their disobedience.

God cherished the qualities of Moses as an effective intercessor for the Israelites. Moses prayed boldly, asking for God's mercy to refrain from divine retribution. In addition, Moses had love and passion for the Lord, showing his prevailing power with Him in prayers. As a result, Moses had a unique opportunity to speak with God face to face.

Though the Bible calls him the meekest man, Moses was fallible. Israel's frequent murmurings and disobedience to God's word exasperated him. He was passionate and impulsive. When God disclosed to Moses that He intended to destroy the nation because the people were worshipping a golden idol at the foot of the Mount Sinai. Moses' response was abrupt when he saw the evil deeds of the people. Enraged, he broke the stone tablets inscribed with God's laws.

Also, Moses failed to obey God when He told him to speak to the rock for water. Because of Moses' irritation with the people's complaints, he struck the rock with his staff instead and violated God's instructions. Therefore, God did not allow him to enter the promised land. Moses' anger and emotions got the best of him. God ordained Moses to deliver His people from bondage and slavery in Egypt. God uses the humble, not the proud. Thus, He humbled him to become the meekest man on earth. Moses teaches us a fundamental lesson to help us morally and spiritually. He had a close relationship with God. Thus, he found confidence in God, and God was with him.

We must follow God's commandments and surrender everything into His hands for him to fight our battles for us. Besides, leadership comes with responsibilities.

The Levitical Priesthood

After God delivered the Israelites from Egypt, the Israelites needed an intercessor because they could not approach God based on their merits. God had made a covenant with them as His people, but they disobeyed the first commandment He gave them. Thus, He separated Aaron and his descendants from the tribe of Levi as priests to minister to Him and stand in the gap for Israel (Exodus 19:6).

> *"12 And take thou unto thee Aaron thy brother, and his sons with him, from among the children of Israel, that he may minister unto me in the priest's office, even Aaron, Nadab and Abihu, Eleazar and Ithamar, Aaron's sons."* — ***Exodus 28:12***

The Levites were a landless Israeli tribe who descended from Levi, a son of Jacob. Aaron was the first son of Jochebed of Levi, Miriam, the oldest, and Moses. God appointed Aaron, an assistant to Moses, was appointed a priest alongside his sons (1 Chronicle 23:13). Aaron became the first high priest of Israel. The rest of the Levites assisted the priests in the tabernacle under the leadership of the priests (Deuteronomy 10:8-9). God allowed only the priests to minister to Him and intercede for Israel.

Some of the Levitical priests include:

- Aaron.
- Eleazar, son of Aaron (Numbers 20:28).
- Phinehas, son of Eleazar.
- Abishua, son of Phinehas.
- Bukki, son of Abishua.
- Uzzi, son of Bukki.
- Ahitub, son of Phinehas.

Samuel, the Prophet, and Judge

The Prophet Samuel was the prophet of God. He was a Levite from the descendants of Kohath. He was also a seer and the last judge of Israel. Samuel led Israel for over forty years and anointed the first king of Israel, Saul, and his successor, David.

Samuel was the son of Elkanah and Hannah. He was born in answer to prayer by his mother, Hannah, at Ramathaim-Zophim in the hill country of Ephraim. Before Samuel was born, his barren mother vowed that if God gave her a son, she would give him back for God's service. So, Hannah dedicated Samuel to God and the care of Eli in Shiloh. He was raised in the house of Eli as a young boy. God revealed Himself to Samuel when he was incredibly young.

God chose Samuel to lead Israel when Eli and his sons failed as priests. Samuel became a mighty prophet and an intercessor for Israel for many years. He challenged Israel to return to the Lord. Samuel interceded in response to God, and the Lord answered him. He warned Israel to serve God since He had chosen them, so they feared the Lord and served Him. Moreover, he warned them not to serve idols since God had desired them to be His possession. He also reminded them of His goodness and to refrain from disobedience, since wickedness attracted punishment.

When Israel requested a king, it displeased Samuel, yet he took their request before God and honored it with a warning. Saul was the first king, but God rejected him since he rebelled. Therefore, God directed Samuel to anoint David as king. Subsequently, God chose the tribe of Judah and established His covenant with the house of David in Israel. He promised David his descendants would sit on Israel's throne until the righteous Branch came to restore His throne (2 Samuel 7:8-16).

45

Isaiah

God chose Isaiah to guide and stand in the gap for Judah to avert the nation from judgment. Judah's kings and priests committed harlotry, just as Israel's backslidden priests did. The priests flouted God's law, despised the holy vessels, showed no difference between the clean and the unclean, and refused to keep the Sabbaths. Judah violated God's word and allied with pagan nations. The prophet Isaiah preached repentance and restoration. He also warned them of God's wrath and chastisement against the ungodly, who did not repent. Isaiah condemned Judah for being unfaithful to God. Judah would go into captivity and return during Cyrus' time, and Jerusalem would be destroyed and rebuilt.

However, Isaiah made persistent prayers and vowed to continue interceding until righteousness was restored in Jerusalem. He recounted God's goodness and reiterated that He was their Father. Isaiah confessed his sins and the sins of his people honestly to God (Isaiah 62:1). Isaiah also had many revelations about the Messiah.

Jeremiah

God commissioned Jeremiah as an intercessor to deliver His words to His people in Israel when he was a youth. Jeremiah doubted his ability to speak because he was young. But God assured him He would be with him and anointed his mouth for the prophetic service over the nations (Jeremiah 1). Israel had turned their back on God and worshipped Baal after all His goodness. Yet Jeremiah preached God's repentance and reminded them of God's love. God had put up with the Israelites' disobedient ways and failure to trust God in its affairs. Jeremiah faithfully to God's word warned the people without fear, but they did not repent. As a result, he often lamented over the people's disobedience to God.

Jeremiah was faithful to God and declared all the words that He told him. When Israel was about to experience God's wrath, he stood before God on Israel's behalf. In his prayers, he confessed they have sinned against God. He confessed their inequities, testified against them, and their rebellion had become many. Jeremiah sought God's mercy to avert judgment. Notwithstanding, his people rejected him. So, Israel suffered God's judgment.

He faced anguish and pain as the people he was helping did not like him and disregarded God's word (Jeremiah 18:20). Some even attempted to kill him, but God protected him. The Lord did not abandon Judah because of His covenant with David. Instead, He spoke to Jeremiah about how He would restore the nation of Israel. We must respond to God's warning and keep seeking Him to remain faithful, even if God does not answer our prayers in the way we desire.

Prophet Daniel

Daniel was humble and obedient, though he was a prince of Judah. He was determined to be holy, even in the hostile environment of Babylonian captivity (Daniel 2). Thus, he decided not to contaminate himself with the food of the Gentile king. As a result, the king honorably assigned him a leadership position. Daniel had a relationship with God and communicated with Him through prayer. He was an intercessor who led a life of devotion to God. He became a vessel and interceded for Israel's restoration (Daniel 9).

When Daniel interceded for the people of Israel, he aligned himself with the sins of his people and confessed their sins. Humbling himself, as there is none righteous, he prayed for God's mercy for Israel.

Furthermore, Daniel, a man of prayer and fasting, prayed not on his own merits, but God's compassion. He also made intercession only for God's glory. He never took God's glory for the many demonstrations of his gifts of dreams and interpretations.

Ezra

Ezra was a descendant of Aaron, the first high priest. He was a priest and a scribe, well-versed in the Law of Moses. Ezra was a compassionate intercessor who lived in Babylon before King Artaxerxes sent him to Jerusalem to teach the laws of God.

When King Cyrus proclaimed the rebuilding of God's Temple in Jerusalem, Zerubbabel led the first volunteers to Jerusalem. After they rebuilt the Temple, Ezra led a large group of exiles back to Jerusalem; he preached to King Artaxerxes about God's goodness and was bold enough to ask the king for help. He trusted God to protect him, and He practiced what he preached. He genuinely grieved over sin.

God, Ezra chose as an intercessor for the Jews. As Ezra walked with God, Ezra had a burden for Judah, who wandered from God's ways. He led the people to return to purity and obey the Lord's commands (Ezra 9).

For example, when he heard that some leaders and priests had married Gentile women contrary to the law of God, he challenged the people to make acceptable sacrifices and get rid of the foreign wives. He submitted his life to God's care to find peace in challenging circumstances. God blessed the Jews with a revival after their exile from Judah, and they began acceptable sacrifices again in the Temple (Ezra 10).

Intercessors in the New Testament

Jesus, the Great High Priest, and Ultimate Intercessor

Jesus is **the only mediator** between God and man, the great high priest and ultimate intercessor. Moreover, the priests and prophets interceded for Israel, but they all had flaws, and some broke the laws. They were mortal, lacked compassion, impure, sinners, and had to confess and atone for their sins with the blood of animals before interceding for others. Moreover, the blood of animals could not make them righteous, as there was a need for repeated daily and seasonal sacrifices for atonement. However, God blessed humanity with the great High Priest, Jesus, the glorified obedient Son. He is the image and likeness of the invisible God. In Him dwells the fullness of the divine attributes of God (Colossians 1:19). He is holy, spotless, compassionate, and blameless.

"For there is one God, and there is one mediator between God and men, the man Christ Jesus." — 1 Timothy 2:5

When Jesus arrived at the opportune time, He achieved what Israel's priests and prophets could not; He atoned for our sin with His spotless blood to reconcile the sinful man and God. He had the perfect ministry of sacrifice and sanctification. He has given us His righteousness. The blood of goats and sheep offered could not purge people from their sins, but the spotless blood that Jesus shed once for us cleansed us from all unrighteousness to serve the living God (Hebrews 9:1-28). The high priest's annual duty on the Day of Atonement was only a shadow of what Jesus eventually did for humanity on the Cross (Romans 8:34). Jesus never sinned. Yet He paid for our sins with His spotless blood once and for all. Jesus is a merciful, faithful, and perfect high priest in the heavens, who fulfilled promises and prophecies foretold by prophets of old. Animal blood sacrifice is no longer necessary required because Jesus shed His blood on the cross of Calvary for the remission of sins (Hebrews 7:2-25; 8:1-13).

Also, Jesus' relationship with God differed from all the priests and prophets as God reconciled the world to Himself through Jesus. He had no sin and was pure (John 1:1-5, 30; 3:16, 17). He is faithful and has a united relationship with God. God forgives our sins through Jesus. Jesus is above all names in Heaven and Earth (Heb. 9:11-15). Our merciful and faithful High Priest became a man and lived like us on earth. So, He understands poverty, temptation, and suffering as a human being, yet He was without sin.

Jesus is **the only priest** qualified to intercede for humanity before God in His own right. He is the truth, life, and the only way to God. Christ is the Word made flesh, the Firstborn from the dead. He is our Creator, Defender, and Redeemer. Christ, the Lord, is greater than the prophets. He is the rock of ages, the sure foundation, the chief cornerstone. Jesus suffered and accepted us as brethren in His humanity and as the seed of Abraham. He defeated the devil. In addition, Jesus is the Apostle and high priest of our soul. He sees everything He had the authority to restore the sick and demon possessed. He protected His disciplines from evil while on Earth. He interceded for all those who would believe in Him so that we would overcome the temptation of Satan. Jesus continues to pray for us as our intercessor in Heaven. He is the reason the presence of God is now amidst His people, our body being God's Temple. His presence manifests as we grow in our faith in Christ by obeying the Word. He commissioned the Church to continue as priests in His stead, both Jews and Gentiles. So, we can boldly come to God through Him in prayer.

The Holy Spirit as Intercessor

Our prayer partner is the Holy Spirit. The privilege of enjoying fellowship with God is through the Son and the Holy Spirit alone. The Holy Spirit, part of the Trinity, has the same attributes of omniscience (all-knowing), omnipresence (present everywhere simultaneously), and unlimited power.

> *"We do not know what we ought to pray for, but the Spirit himself intercedes for us through wordless groans 7 And he that searcheth the hearts knoweth what is the mind of the Spirit, and because he maketh intercession for the saints according to the will of God." — **Romans 8:26***

Jesus assured His disciples with the help of the Holy Spirit to continue His ministry on earth. On the day of Pentecost, God fulfilled this promise. This day commemorates the Holy Spirit's outpouring and empowerment of the Apostles and other disciples to proclaim the gospel to the world. The Holy Spirit only came on the righteous periodically in the Old Testament. He possesses emotions, intellect, and will and dwells in the children of God until Jesus returns (John 14:26).

The Holy Spirit is our *Comforter, Counselor, Advocate Strengthener, Intercessor, and Guide. The Holy Ghost, Counselor, and the Spirit of Truth* are other names of the Holy Spirit.

- He consoles, intercedes, and performs things that only God can perform, such as creation, regeneration, and sanctification, and assures us of salvation.
- Further, the Holy Spirit speaks to us and causes the truth to be explicit.

51

- He guides and directs our lives with His impartation.

- In addition, the Holy Spirit strengthens our thoughts and enables us to pray according to God's will.

- Finally, he helps the believer live victoriously over sin and guides us through our struggles.

People who place their faith in Jesus Christ and respond to his conviction will receive eternal life and a new nature.

- The Holy Spirit empowers us with spiritual gifts to witness; it empowers and imparts spiritual gifts to witness.

- Whether a holy assignment or a national calamity, the Spirit helps the believer carry the burden placed upon them.

- The Holy Spirit intercedes for us and allows us to intervene. He is the Spirit of Truth, who teaches the word of God with divine revelations. The Holy Spirit is an intercessor and our guide as we yield to Him. He helps us and shows us things to come (John 14:16).

- Further, He intercedes for believers based on the will of God when we do not know how or what to pray.

- Finally, he is everyone's most dependable ally in times of trouble. The disciples relied on Him in difficult situations.

An intercessor follows the lead of the Holy Spirit and waits for His guidance (Romans 8:26-27).

First, the Holy Spirit helps us pray in times of great difficulty.

Then, when we do not have the words to pray, He groans on our behalf as he intercedes for us before God.

Intercessors in the Early Church
Apostle Peter

As a new creation in Christ and with the empowerment of the Holy Spirit, the believers in the early church became faithful intercessors.

Peter was the disciple of Jesus. He and his brother Andrew were fishers, and their calling occurred when Jesus met them casting their nets. Jesus said to them, "Follow me, and I will make you fishers of men" (Matthew 4:18). Meaning they would preach the word and bring others into the kingdom of God (Ephesians 2:20-22).

Jesus gave Peter and the other disciples the power to intercede for the people as they preached the gospel (Matthew 10:5-40). They prayed to heal the sick and delivered others from unclean spirits. Additionally, when Jesus ascended, they all went to Jerusalem to receive the Holy Spirit, as instructed by Jesus, "tarry ye in the city of Jerusalem, until ye be endued with power from on high." (Luke 24:49).

After receiving the Spirit, Peter taught the people and reproved their actions, with about three thousand saved in one day. Finally, he interceded, and a blind man received his sight (Acts 2, 3). Moreover, he also prayed for Aeneas, who had been sick with palsy for eight years. Peter said, "Jesus Christ maketh thee whole," and Jesus, through Peter, healed Aeneas.

After Jesus chose Peter to lead the church, he performed many works recorded in the Bible. Though Peter denied Jesus when He was arrested, he repented and fulfilled his ministry to lead the church.

The Apostle Paul

Paul persecuted and jailed Christians spreading the gospel of Christ with the connivance of the authorities. He agreed and witnessed the stoning to the death of Stephen. One day, when he was on his way to arrest more Christians in Damascus, he encountered Jesus, and a shiny light from heaven suddenly showed around him. Then he fell to the ground and heard a voice saying,

"Saul, Saul, why are you persecuting me?" (Acts 9:4).

He became blind and the people accompanying Saul led him to Damascus, and for three days, he fasted.

Furthermore, the Lord sent Ananias to pray for Paul. After that, Paul stayed with the Lord's followers in Damascus, where he went to the Synagogue and preached about Christ. Everyone who heard Paul's preaching was surprised because they had listened to what he had done to the followers of Christ. Paul preached with power and authority, which surprised the Jewish people in Damascus.

Later, some of them planned to kill Paul. But when he heard of it, he escaped to Jerusalem to be with the Lord's followers. However, they feared him because they did not believe he was authentic.

Subsequently, God chose Paul and Barnabas as partners, and the Church in Antioch prayed for them to go on their way to preach. Paul traveled extensively to preach the word. Unfortunately, the Jewish people became jealous of Paul and maltreated him. Despite all Paul's troubles, he was ready to die for Christ.

Ananias

Ananias was a believer in Damascus. He was a devout observer of the law and highly respected by all the Jews living there. God sent Ananias to intercede for Saul (Paul) to regain his eyesight because he became blind during an encounter with Jesus on his way to Damascus to arrest Christians (Acts 9:1-9). Ananias was not willing to do what God had instructed because he knew of the evil Saul had done to the followers of Christ. But God assured him He had appointed Saul as His chosen servant to preach the name of Jesus to many.

> *[15] But the Lord said unto him, Go thy way: for he is a chosen vessel unto me, to bear my name before the Gentiles, and kings, and the children of Israel: — Acts 9:17*

So, Ananias obeyed God and went on his way to where Saul was lodging. Then, Ananias laid his hands on Saul and prayed for him as God had instructed.

> *"And Ananias went his way and entered into the house; and putting his hands on him said, Brother Saul, the Lord, even Jesus, that appeared unto thee in the way as thou camest, hath sent me, that thou mightest receive thy sight, and be filled with the Holy Ghost." — Acts 9:17*

Saul regained his sight. Then Ananias baptized Saul, therefore, converting him to Christianity. The man who persecuted believers now depends on one.

Intercessors Today

The Israelites could not enter the Holy place to offer their sacrifice since only the Levitical priests could come into God's presence. In contrast, believers come directly to God in the New Testament through the great High Priest, Jesus Christ. So, there are no earthly mediators between God and men. Jesus, our High Priest, made one sacrifice for the sin of all men, and no sacrifices are required anymore.

When Jesus died, God tore the veil of the Temple, allowing us direct access to the holy place where we could receive mercy. Therefore, when we confess and accept Jesus as our Savior, we become a part of God's royal priesthood and gain the privilege of coming to the Father in prayer for ourselves and others.

God uses believers as a kingdom of priests to represent Him in the ministry of intercession. According to the Bible, Jesus has made every believer a royal priest of God. Jesus fulfilled the law and dedicated all believers as the kings and priests of God. Thus, believers have unrestricted access to the holiest of all to offer the sacrifices of praise and thanksgiving (1 Peter 2:9-10).

So also, believers are God's treasured possession, the chosen royal Priests, delivered from the darkness, called to be holy and blameless in His sight, to proclaim His excellence.

> *"[1] I exhort, therefore, that, first of all, supplications, prayers, intercessions, and giving of thanks, be made for all men; [2] For kings, and for all that are in authority; that we may lead a quiet and peaceable life in all godliness and honesty." — 1* **Tim. 2:1-2**

We are supposed to fulfill all His will, offer spiritual sacrifices, and proclaim the praises of Him who delivered us from darkness into His light. The believer's body is the Temple of the Holy Spirit, and our heart is the altar (1 Corinthians 6:19-20). So, God has commissioned us to present our beings as living sacrifices, serving Him from our hearts (Romans 12:1-2). God, through Christ, reconciled the world to himself. Additionally, He has given believers the duty to **continue the ministry of reconciliation**.

> *"[18] And all things are of God, who has reconciled us to himself by Jesus Christ, and has given to us the ministry of reconciliation; [19] To wit, that God was in Christ, reconciling the world unto himself not imputing their trespasses unto them, and has committed unto us the word of reconciliation. [20] Now then we are ambassadors for Christ as though God beseech you by us, we pray you in Christ stead be reconciled to God." — 2 Corinthians 5:18-20*

Every believer must praise God for the redemption that came through Jesus Christ and live a well-pleasing life that brings honor and glory to Him. We must declare his Lordship to the people around us and pray for those in darkness to come into the light by helping them see the glorious nature of Jesus. The Holy Scriptures encourage believers of Christ to approach the throne of God in times of need (Hebrews 16:22). We must allow Him to strengthen us in prayer. The divine calling of intercession will accomplish His plans on Earth as in Heaven (1 John 5:1). Furthermore, God can inspire our hearts to stand in the gap for people, families, and countries. Therefore, we must heed the call and move with compassion and mercy to pray for God's intervention, grace, and protection to save souls from danger.

In Conclusion

Intercessory prayer is a petition to God for His mercy to restore. Today, God seeks intercessors, since all believers of Christ have been drafted into the ministry of intercession and reconciliation. Jesus paid the price for our redemption, but humanity is perishing in darkness. Therefore, God desires us to rise and intercede for others.

Readers must understand that God chose and consecrated only the priests and prophets to stand in the gap for His people under the Old Testament.

However, in **the New Testament**, Christ Jesus paid the sacrificial price as the ultimate intercessor.

- He is humanity's ultimate advocate and intercessor before God's throne.
- He has made believers God's royal priests and intercessors.

As today's believers and tomorrow's intercessors, you must stand in the gap in prayer for others. We have the Holy Spirit as our helper to come before God's throne, repenting and confessing our sins, asking for forgiveness for the communities in humility.

What standard does God demand from his called vessels? We will discuss some qualities of intercessors in the following chapter.

3

Qualities of an Intercessor

Believers have the mandate to pray for others, but what qualities make us **effective intercessors**? Intercessors must have **godly qualities** to be effective in the ministry of intercession. God always sets the divine standard for **His chosen servants** for effective ministry. His prophets, the Levitical priests as intercessors in the Old Testament, led a holy life, separated from sinners, obedient, merciful, and having complete devotion strictly to His laws since none can come to God with uncleanness. Yet, they broke some of God's laws.

"Holiness, without which no one will see the Lord."—Heb. 12:14

However, Jesus, the **flawless son** of God, and the exact radiance of God's glory and the exact depiction of His nature, is the only perfect intercessor (Matthew 16:16). In His earthly ministry, Jesus reflected the character of God and exhibited godly qualities such as love, peace, compassion, patience, and obedience. Jesus had an intimate fellowship with God, and He never sinned. He has empowered every believer as an intercessor with the Holy Spirit to live a godly life to bear the fruits of the spirit. So, intercessors follow the way of the master, Jesus, to maintain a close relationship with God and exhibit godly traits such as holiness, loving obedience to His word, complete devotion, and many more.

Qualification of intercessors in the Old Testament

The Levitical Priesthood

God established the mandatory priesthood by birth from the family of Aaron in Israel as intercessors for Israel. He gave them laws through Moses to govern their lifestyle. Among others, God required the priesthood to have the following qualities.

- Holiness.
- Blameless and unblemished by God's standard.
- Separation from Sinners.
- Obedience.
- Complete Devotion.

Holiness

God is perfect and free of all evil and flaws, and no one can approach Him with uncleanness. He demands His servants to separate themselves from the uncleanness of the world. He desires service from a holy heart because He is holy. So, when God appeared to Abraham after Ishmael was born, He said, "I am God Almighty; Walk before Me and be ye thou perfect" (Genesis 17:1). So, Abraham obeyed and intimately knew God. He built altars and worshiped Him. Likewise, Job was an upright man who feared God and shunned evil, though his three friends accused him.

When God chose Aaron and his sons as priests, He commanded them to be holy by observing all the rules He gave to Moses. That no one shall make himself unclean for the dead among his people, except for his closest relatives. A husband must be clean among his people and not profane himself, nor offer unblemished sacrifices. They must not marry a prostitute or a woman who has been defiled, neither shall they marry a woman divorced from her husband, for the priest is holy to his God among others.

The chief priest must not let the hair of his head hang loose nor tear his clothes. No man of the offspring of Aaron the priest who has a blemish must come near to offer the Lord's food offerings; since he has a blemish, he shall not come near to offer the bread of his God and many more.

They also washed with water, wore holy garments, and offered sacrifices for their sins before appearing to Him in the temple to pray for Israel (Exodus 30:19-21).

> *"I am the Lord your God; consecrate yourselves and be holy, because I am holy." — **Leviticus 11:44***

God's holy nature abhors sin, and His righteous judgment comes upon those who violate His sacred laws. So, He punished those who defiled themselves and His holy temple. For instance, the high priest would die if he entered the holy place unclean. The two sons of Aaron died in the tabernacle because they disobeyed protocols and offered strange fire before the Lord.

> *Be careful that you do not forget the Lord your God, failing to observe his commands, laws, and decrees that I am giving you this day—- **Deuteronomy 8:11***

When Israel defiled the Temple with idols, God's presence left the temple, and their enemies destroyed the temple. An obvious demonstration that God will not entertain uncleanness in His presence. He also rejected the sacrifices of the priests who defiled themselves with Gentile women.

Blameless

Blameless, in Scripture, refers to those who are innocent of offense and without guilt — integrity, truth, perfect, sincere, undefiled, upright, whole, spotless, obedient, and unblemished.

> *"²He that walketh uprightly, and worketh righteousness, and speaketh the truth in his heart. ³He that backbiteth not with his tongue, nor doeth evil to his neighbor, nor taketh up a reproach against his neighbour." — **Psalm 15:2-3***

God is blameless in all His ways, including His judgments. He does no wrong and is never at fault. God commands His servants to be blameless because our faithfulness honors Him. Noah was blameless and did good things that set him apart from the rest of humanity. He was a righteous man, innocent among the people of his time, and walked faithfully with God (Genesis 6:9). Likewise, Job was blameless and upright before God (Job 1:1).

> *"You shall be perfect with the LORD your God." — **Deuteronomy 18:13***

God commanded the priests to be blameless and perform their duties in sincerity. He required them to judge the people according to the law and not defraud them. For instance, God punished the sons of Eli the high priest for their fraudulent deals with sacrifices. They took portions of sacrifices belonging to the Lord and despised the offerings (1 Samuel 2:12-17). Similarly, when David committed adultery with Beersheba and killed her husband, God told David he had given occasion to others to blaspheme His name. Only those who walk blamelessly and righteously, who speak the truth from their heart will dwell in God's tent and will never be shaken (Psalm 15).

Separation from Sinners

God commanded His people to cleave unto Him and be separated from sinners and the worldly system so that ungodly people would not influence them to serve other gods. For instance, God told Abraham to leave his kindred and travel to a land He would direct him. He also commanded the Israelites not to marry the Baal-worshipping Canaanites, or else they would ensnare them in idolatry. When Solomon married Gentile women, they lured him into idolatry (Deuteronomy 7:3-8; Exodus 34:15-17, 1 Kings 11:1-6). David also spoke about separation from sinners when He said, "I do not sit with deceitful men, nor do I consort with hypocrites." (Psalm 26:4).

> *"¹And the LORD spake unto Moses in the plains of Moab by Jordan near Jericho, saying, ²Command the children of Israel, that they give unto the Levites of the inheritance of their possession cities to dwell in; and ye shall give also unto the Levites suburbs for the cities round about them. ³And the cities shall they have to dwell in; and the suburbs of them shall be for their cattle, and for their goods, and for all their beasts."* — **Numbers 35:1-4**

God physically separated the tribe of Levi from the rest of the Israelites when He chose them to minister before Him. He gave the Levites their cities separate from the rest of the host tribes. Thus, the priests dwelt together, and the Levites lived together in cities, given to them by the rest of the tribes of Israel. When Israel defiled the Temple with idols, God's presence left the temple, and their enemies destroyed the temple. An obvious demonstration that God will not entertain uncleanness in His presence. Similarly, God rejected the sacrifices of the priests who defiled themselves with Gentile women.

Obedience

God requires His faithful servants to obey His Word in His way and time. He rewards obedience with blessings that bring rest to our souls. He has elevated His word above His name and demands total obedience to His word. For example, Abraham believed and obeyed God, and for this, God blessed him, and he was called a friend of God (Genesis 18). His outstanding quality was his faith and obedience to God. When God asked him to leave his father's house for an unknown destination, he obeyed God's command without hesitation. Additionally, he obeyed God to sacrifice his son, but God provided a ram in his son's stead as he was about to sacrifice him. He believed God would provide.

Also, Moses was an example of someone who obeyed God's laws in the face of vast challenges, as he had great faith in God. He had the boldness and the will to risk his own life for Israel. Moses obediently led the Israelites out of Egypt through the Red Sea. God commanded decreed the Levitical priests to obey all the laws Moses gave them.

Also, Samuel was obedient as he followed Eli's instructions, even when God called him in his youth. He encouraged Israel to follow the Lord and held people accountable for disobedience. Samuel was faithful to God and honest when he dispensed God's law. Also, whatever God told him, he passed it on to the people (1 Samuel 9:27). Daniel was humble and obedient. He was determined to obey the commandments of God, even in the hostile pagan environment of Babylonian captivity (Daniel 2). He decided not to defile himself with the food of the Gentile king. Thus, God honored him by raising him to leadership positions and giving him a long life with the gift of interpreting dreams and visions. He became a vessel and interceded for Israel's restoration (Daniel 9).

Complete Devotion

Intercessors must give up personal comforts for God's mission. Total dedication is the only way to serve God faithfully. Abraham left his kindred in Mesopotamia for Canaan. He obediently prepared to sacrifice his son Isaac when God asked him to. After Isaac was bound to an altar, God saw his willingness and furnished him with a sacrificial lamb in Isaac's stead. A messenger from God stopped Abraham before the sacrifice, saying, "now I know you fear God" (Genesis 22:1-19). Abraham looked up, saw a ram, and sacrificed it.

Moses had to carry the burden of Israel throughout their forty-year journey from Egypt to Canaan. They even threatened to stone him, but he was dedicated to God's mission.

God consecrated the Levitical priests and the Levites for complete devotion to His service. They did not do any work aside from their priesthood duties, and God provided for their needs by giving them portions of the offerings and sacrifices.

However, some priests, like the sons of Eli, abused these privileges, denied justice, and defrauded the people. False prophets gave fake visions contrary to God's word. For instance, they assured the people of hope, contrary to Jeremiah's warning that the Babylonians would capture Jerusalem.

This happened after some priests defiled the vessels of the Temple and disregarded the Sabbath, made no apparent distinction between the sacred and the profane in the temple, and worshipped idols. They also mistreated their wives, widows, orphans, and oppressed strangers.

Qualification of Intercessors in the New Testament

Jesus, the Ultimate Intercessor

The Old Testament intercessors had imperfections. So, at the proper time, God sent His only Son, Jesus, as the perfect high priest for Jews and Gentiles. Jesus was holy, blameless, and separated from sinners (Hebrews 7:26-28).

First, God anointed Jesus as the Messiah with an eternal mandate (Hebrews 7:1-21). Second, His priesthood was based on God's promise of redemption to all men through Abraham. Third, he offered Himself once before the Lord as a sacrificial lamb for us (Matthew 27:46). So, He does not need to atone for our sins daily as the Levitical priests did for Israel. Also, He can save those who come to God through Him for eternity. Jesus now sits at the Father's right hand as the great High Priest, interceding for humanity. As our role model, Jesus exhibited the following qualities as the ultimate intercessor:

- Relationship with God.
- Holiness.
- Blameless.
- Separation from the world.
- Obedience.
- Complete Devotion.

Relationship with the Father

The Trinity comprises three persons: the Father, the Son, and the Holy Spirit. Jesus had a unique relationship with His heavenly Father. He was obedient and united with God as He did things to please His Father while on earth. He was one with Father in everything He did (John 10:30). Jesus is the *image* and the radiance of God's glorious nature, upholding all things by His powerful word. He showed the elements of God's character, such as love, holiness, omnipotence, just, grace, and mercy. He had a perfect relationship with God because they are One. Moreover, Jesus is the only mediator between God and man because He alone could go to God in His own right to plead for us. Jesus usually withdrew Himself from the people to commune with. God, whose presence was always with Him.

*"Come near to God and He will come near to you." — **James 4:7***

Jesus *depended* on his Father. He did nothing of his own accord, though He was equal with the Father. Everything He did was according to God's word. Jesus submitted to His Father as a son and obeyed all His laws, walking in humility before His Father. Also, He believed in His Father's love and lived for His will. His intimate relationship with God was the source of His love, compassion, grace, wisdom, anointing, and power needed for His earthly ministry (John 20:17, Mat. 27:46). Jesus did nothing by Himself, but only did what He saw His Father do. "For the Father loves the Son and showed the son what He was doing" (John 5:20).

Jesus also showed His works to the disciples on Earth. He worked with God to give life. He sought not His will but the will of Him who sent Him, and God validated Him (Matthew 3:13-17). Also, God honored Him, gave Him a name above all names, and committed everything to His hands. As a result, He sits at the Father's right hand on High as an intercessor for humanity (Heb. 1:3,13). His disciples depended on Him for the words of eternal life. They loved and had faith in Him. Jesus revealed the Father to them, which was reflected in their ministry after His departure. Through Jesus' introduction of God as the Father, the disciples experienced a new relationship with God.

Effective intercession is rooted in a relationship with God through Jesus. We must receive Jesus as our Savior and submit to His lordship by obeying His laws. From our position as His children in Christ, we talk with Him, meditate on His Word, and take part in His work on earth. Thus, every intercessor must have a personal and nurturing relationship with God through Jesus. Jesus is the only way to God. The highest value of God's Kingdom is relationship. He shares His heart with intercessors when we pray for His will to be done on earth. He rewards our trust and faith with power, strength, love, knowledge, and peace.

> [18] *No man hath seen God at any time, the only begotten Son, which is in the bosom of the Father, he hath declared him.* [19] *And this is the record of John, when the Jews sent priests and Levites from Jerusalem to ask him, Who art thou?* — ***John 1:18***

Therefore, we must obey the greatest and first commandment: to love God with all our heart, soul, and mind by surrendering to Him. We must fellowship daily by reading and obeying the Word, praising, and worshipping Him. Our priority in prayer should always be fellowship with the Father. Our relationship with God must reflect in our relationship with people. There must be good neighborliness and a harmonious relationship, kindness, and mercy. Also, love, honor, and respect for our parents and siblings enhance our relationship with God. Sin separates us from God, but repentance restores our relationship with Him. Jesus, our mediator, restored the fellowship that Adam and Eve lost in the Garden of Eden. Therefore, God accepts us with open hands as His children when we accept Jesus as our Lord.

Holiness

Jesus is the holy Son of God. The Holy Spirit conceived Jesus to become the only begotten Son of God — sacred to the Lord for our sake.

> *"What do you want with us, Jesus of Nazareth? Have you come to destroy us? I know who you are the Holy One of God!" — **Mark 1:24***

Holiness means separation from the profane — the world of sin, darkness, and evil. God is holy and perfect in all His ways and has a perpetual intolerance for sin. Human effort to know Him is fruitless because of His eminence, but He reveals Himself to man through Jesus. He is the Holy Father. His name, laws, and covenants are holy. So, His angels, prophets, and elects must be holy.

> *"How much more shall the blood of Christ, who through the eternal Spirit offered himself without spot to God, purge your conscience from dead works to serve the living God?" — **Hebrews 9:14***

> *"Then spake Jesus again unto them, saying, I am the light of the world: he that followeth me shall not walk in darkness, but shall have the light of life." — **John 8:12***

Christ's holiness manifested in His love for righteousness and hatred of iniquity and evil. He was perfect and spotless, so He loved the righteous and reproved man's iniquity, including the priests and the Pharisees.

> *"Thou hast loved righteousness, and hated iniquity; therefore God, even thy God, hath anointed thee with the oil of gladness above thy fellows." — **Hebrews 1:9***

Christ showed holiness in deed and word; He never sinned nor spoke a lie, though the Jews tempted and harassed Him many times. Instead, He did everything according to the Father's will (John 12:49). His holy nature manifested itself in constant victory over temptation.

Though Satan tempted Him to deviate from God's plan by abusing His authority, He remained devoted to God. He used the Scriptures to resist all such temptations (Hebrews 4:15; Matthew 4:1-11). Similarly, He demanded absolute perfection in His disciples without compromise (Matthew 5:48). He scathingly rebuked sin, though He showed compassion to sinners. He saved people from their sins and counseled them to be righteous to escape eternal damnation (1 Peter 2:24; Matthew 25:31-32). Even unclean spirits discerned Jesus as the "Holy One of God" (Mark 1:24).

He sanctified Himself and the apostles with the truth (John 17:19). He resurrected from the dead because the grave could not keep Him (Psalm 16:30). Jesus is holy, yet He sympathizes with our struggles. Therefore, intercessors, as new creations in Christ born of water and the Holy Spirit, must be holy to worship God in spirit and truth. We pursue holiness with all our hearts since, without holiness, no one can see God. God expects us to be holy because He does not mix the pure with the profane. His Word says holiness glorifies Him because He is Holy.

Holiness is the core of God's divine nature. God is Holy, and He is without sin in His nature. He is sinless and cannot overlook our sin in any form, such as anger, bitterness, strife, fornication, adultery, idolatry, pride, unforgiveness, and more (Gal. 5:18-21). He judges sin because justice comes from His holiness. However, He gives grace when we repent.

70

Consequently, we must hate what is evil and confess our petrifying sin to be forgiven. He demands a pure relationship through Jesus. His holiness demands that we forsake our sinful inclinations to appropriate His goodness, since things that belong to Him are sacred (Romans 12:1-2).

We must obey the Scriptures and dwell in His presence under the Lordship of Holy Jesus, so our actions and attitude will please God (1 Corinthians 7:1). [Enter your work phone number here]

We must forsake and confess generational sins and iniquities so He can hear our prayers. Jesus offers divine redemption and daily transformation for the unrighteous, ungodly, and unclean but does not expect us to return to worldly lusts. The Bible entreats us to thank God and implore Him for deliverance from evil (1 Thessalonians. 2:10-13).

> *"14 As obedient children, not fashioning yourselves according to the former lusts in your ignorance:15 But as he which hath called you is holy, so be ye holy in all manner of conversation;16 because it is written, Be ye holy; for I am holy." — 1 Peter 1:14-16*

All forms of evil and uncleanness, such as a bitter and unforgiving spirit, hinder prayers, and fellowship with God. Jesus said, "But if ye forgive not men their trespasses, neither will your Father forgive your trespasses" (Matthew 6:15). If we are bitter or unforgiving, He will not hear our prayers.

Therefore, we must allow God to handle our pain, as He is our vindicator and judge. Jesus forgave and prayed for those who crucified Him.

Blameless

Jesus' nature is eternally sinless, as He lived perfectly with God before coming to earth. His earthly life was perfect without sin (Mat 4:1-10). He ascended to God and lives in perfection. Jesus is pure in heart, blameless, and free from sin and guilt. His victory over sin and temptation proved He was divine. He was steadfast in spirit, focusing solidly on God's will and His love for man.

Moreover, Jesus had no volatility and doubt; instead, He had harmony, peace, and stability. The Son of God was always willing to do the will of His heavenly Father (John 14:30). Everything Jesus did and said was in obedience to God. He had pure motives with a united heart with God. He completed God's will for His glory. A genuine soul hates evil and serves God wholeheartedly, even amid trials.

> *"For we do not have a high priest who cannot sympathize with our weaknesses, but one who in every respect has been tempted as we are, yet without sin." — **Hebrews 7:26***

Jesus' accusers tried in vain to find any evil against Him. The chief priests and the Pharisees brought false witnesses to testify against Him, but their testimonies were inconsistent as He was innocent. He did not steal or defraud any man.

Neither did He seek the glory and praise of man. He did not reply when they insulted, beat, and condemned Him without cause. Jesus had authority over the enemy because there was no deceit in Him (John 14:30). He is the mediator between the imperfect man and the holy God because He paid for our sins with His spotless blood. Thus, Jesus is the savior, way, truth, and life; without Him, no one can see God (John 14:6).

Like Jesus, intercessors must be blameless before God and man. We must serve with a pure heart. Intercessors get a pure heart by consecration and obedience to the Word. Our words and deeds must be in line with the word of God. Any sin is a matter of the heart, which requires cleansing. A pure heart is essential for effective intercession.

> *"Blessed are the pure in heart, for they shall see God." —*
> ***Matthew 5:8***

Only God can cleanse our hearts as we submit to Him. We must confess our sins and obey His Word. The Bible says those with clean hands, pure hearts, and without vanity can seek the face of God. Pursuing righteousness leads to a pure heart. So, we must consistently examine our walk with God to be blameless before Him and man. Intercessors must pray for their souls to become hungry and thirsty for righteousness.

> *"The good man brings good things out of the good treasure of his heart, and the evil man brings evil things out of the evil treasure of his heart. For out of the overflow of the heart, the mouth speaks." — **Luke 6:45***

Therefore, we must avoid sins of the heart, such as anger, greed, bitterness, rage, jealousy, and hatred. These manifest in our decisions, actions, and expressions as we become legalistic and self-righteous, with a routine form of duty devoid of passion for Christ's service.

Thus, our prayers to affect lives become words without power, and we lose the focus of our divine purpose and pay attention to things of no eternal value. Only Jesus can bring it all out and create a clean heart and a renewed spirit for us to pray from a genuine heart as we surrender to Him.

Separated from sinners

Jesus was separate from sinners in the heart. He was morally perfect, filled with pure thoughts, and quick to discern the right. Yet, he was meek and humble in heart. He always submitted to the will of God. Jesus did not deny His divinity, yet He dined and preached to sinners to save the lost.

> *"For such an high priest became us, who is holy, harmless, undefiled, separate from sinners, and made higher than the heavens." — Hebrews 7:26-28*

As an intercessor, He did not come to call the righteous, but sinners to repent. The self-righteous could not receive His gospel. He reached out to save sinners like Zacchaeus and the Samaritan woman. Jesus delivered the adulterous woman from death and the demon-possessed, like Mary Magdalene, who became a committed follower.

God wants believers and intercessors to be separated from the worldly system, separated from sin, and consecrated to God for a sacred purpose. Jesus never condoned their sins.

> *"Wherefore come ye out from among them, and be ye separate, saith the Lord, and touch no unclean thing; and I will receive." — 2 Corinthians 6:17*

God wants us to preach and pray for non-believers, but He does not want His children to associate with their ungodliness. We are God's temple and should have nothing to do with darkness.

> *"Be not unequally yoked with unbelievers: for what fellowship have righteousness and iniquity? or what communion hath light with darkness? And what concord hath*

Christ with Belial? or what portion hath a believer with an unbeliever? And what agreement hath a temple of God with idols? for we are a temple of the living God; even as God said, I will dwell in them, and walk in them; and I will be their God, and they shall be my people. Wherefore Come ye out from among them, and be ye separate, saith the Lord, And touch no unclean thing; And I will receive you, And will be to you a Father, And ye shall be to me sons and daughters, saith the Lord Almighty." — **2 Corinthians 6:14**

Paul told the Corinthians to be cautious about the "so-called" believers who claim to be Christian but live contrary to what the Bible says.

"11But now I have written unto you not to keep company, if any man that is called a brother be a fornicator, or covetous, or an idolater, or a railer, or a drunkard, or an extortioner; with such an one no not to eat. 12For what have I to do to judge them also that are without? do not ye judge them that are within? 13But them that are without God judgeth. Therefore put away from among yourselves that wicked person." — **1 Corinthians 5:11-13**

The command simply means to be separated from sin. Sin and holiness are the reasons Jesus died, and He expects all believers to obey and follow His teachings by forsaking sin and living a holy life.

Obedience

Obedience is the surest way to worship and glorify God. It is the only way to show love, respect, and growth in our relationship with Him. God created man to take care of all creations and rule over the Earth. Our obedience shows gratitude for the blessings given to us. Jesus was obedient to God's will and His laws without failure, including a shameful death for the salvation of humanity.

He submitted to His Father and was free of sin and compromise. God rewards obedience. Because Jesus was in total submission to Him, God exalted Him and gave Him everything (Philippians 2:9-11). Thus, the authority of the name of Jesus causes every knee, situation, and circumstance to submit and bow in reverence in the heavenly, earthly, and demonic realms.

Jesus is our example of submitting to God's will for abundant blessing, peace, joy, love, and patience. Besides, fruitful prayers depend on obedience to God's Word and His spiritual authority over those who obey His commands. Total submission to God and His spiritual authority is the key to effective intercession. Powerful intercessors surrender to God's will and purpose through Jesus. Hence, prayer and obedience work together. For His Word says, if we remain in Him and His words remain in us, He will grant our desires. Intercessors have power and authority when they submit to God through Jesus. Unless we abide in Him and obey His laws, we cannot do anything nor bear fruit. When we rebel, we fall into the hands of the enemy with dire consequences (Luke 6:29-37).

Besides, God blesses our righteousness and obedience as intercessors by answering our prayers. Thus, we must surrender in full obedience to the word of God.

Complete Devotion

God commands us to dedicate ourselves to serving Him wholeheartedly. We show our devotion to God through zealous affection - openly yielding our hearts to Him in reverence, service, faith, and holiness. God desires His people to serve Him alone. Thus, He abhors idolatry. Jesus left His glorious abode in heaven to become a humble sacrifice so that we might share in His glory and enjoy eternal life with His Father. He did all these out of total devotion to God and to accomplish God's mission (John 4:34).

> *"14That we henceforth be no more children, tossed to and fro, and carried about with every wind of doctrine, by the sleight of men, and cunning craftiness, whereby they lie in wait to deceive; 15But speaking the truth in love, may grow up into him in all things, which is the head, even Christ:"* — ***Ephesians 4:14-15***

In the same way, the apostles devotedly preached the gospel, though they faced threats from the Pharisees. The Jews killed and imprisoned some of the early Christians, but they shared their experiences as they evangelized, warning people to repent. So likewise, the Christian life is a commitment to God through Jesus Christ. We grow closer to Him as our relationship deepens through dedicated service and prayer (1 Thessalonian 5:17). We must show Christ in every aspect of our lives and be aware of His presence. The Holy Spirit is our dependable counselor and guides us into the truth. He will lead us to serve God in spirit and truth as we dedicate ourselves to His service. Denominational and man's doctrine will lead to idolatry. For instance, Saul followed the wrong doctrine to persecute the church, thinking he was serving God. Therefore, intercessors must devote themselves to reading and teaching God's word.

Other traits Jesus exhibited — Love

Jesus Christ loved the Father as the Father loved Him (John 3:35; 10:17; 14:31). Compassionate love considers the well-being of others. It affectionately aims to ease suffering and foster others' welfare. Divine love or agape is pure love that only God can give. It expresses God's deep compassion for everyone, including the unworthy. Recipients of this love also love God and help others seek Him.

Jesus' love for the Father manifested itself in His total obedience to His commandments (John 14:21), including giving up heaven's glory for earth's shame. Jesus loved the Father and submitted to His will even when He died on the cross. His death was voluntary in the highest sense. It was a mission Jesus sacrificially accomplished for the Father and His love for humanity. Even as a youth, doing the Father's will and completing His work was Jesus Christ's focus (Luke 2:49). He sought the Father's will, accepting testimony and glory from the Father alone, not men.

Besides, Jesus Christ loved believers. He cherished all those who believed in Him and kept His commandments. Jesus also loved sinners, His enemies, children, and the humble. He forgave when people repented and believed in Him. He sought the lost sheep and cared for them, healing infirmities and sicknesses (Mark 1:41;)

God's perfect love is a fruit that results from obedience to His word. Jesus is a high priest who empathizes with our infirmities because He was tempted, like us, but without sin. Further, He understands our weaknesses and is sympathetic to our battle against the flesh. He gave Himself to humanity out of God's love (John 3:16). Jesus worked out of love for the Father and man. He did nothing without love, stating that it was worthless to do anything without it. He taught people to love their enemies, saying, "But I say unto you which hear, Love your enemies, do good to them which hate you, Bless them that curse you, and pray for them which despitefully use you." (Luke 6:27-28). Also, He forgave His persecutors, including the crucifiers.

Belief in the love of God for us and others helps us pray for those who do not know Him. We may have different views about others, but God's heart is always redemptive (1 Peter 4:8). Jesus mercifully went through all the towns and villages, preaching the good news of the kingdom in the synagogues, healing every disease, and setting captives free. When He saw the crowds following Him, He had compassion for them because they were helpless like sheep without a shepherd (Matthew 9:35-38). He loved us all. Jesus taught us God's love in the parable of the "prodigal son." A rich man's son gained his inheritance and departed from his father to a far country where he led a riotous life, leading to poverty and deprivation. After a while and through hardship, he resolved to return to his father's house. When the Father saw him, he was moved with compassion and welcomed him home (Luke 15:11). God still yearns for our return after we make mistakes. Christ laid down His life to save sinners.

Similarly, effective intercessors must love the people they pray for. The love of the Father motivates intercessors to pray for those who do not know Him. If we stand in the gap in anger, revenge, and ungodly control, then God will not answer. He only responds to love and obedience to the scriptures. Jesus commanded us to pray for our enemies and not for harm to come upon them. Always pray in love, and do not rejoice that something terrible happened or could happen to a person we want to judge (1 Corinthians 13). So intercessors must not judge or condemn those they pray for.

Sacrificial Life

God requires us to give up our desires for His sake and others.

The most joyful people sacrifice for other people wholeheartedly. This type of sacrifice should be in the hearts of intercessors as they pray for others.

> [33] *"So likewise, whosoever he be of you that forsaketh not all that he hath, he cannot be my disciple," — **Luke 14:33.***

Jesus set an example of sacrifice for us to emulate. He left His heavenly glory and waded into the earthly realm laden with sin to save man. He sacrificed His life and everything to restore the broken relationship between God and man. We have access to the Father because Jesus paid the price for our sins with His sinless blood.

Additionally, Jesus taught sacrificial intercession when He said, "Even as the Son of man came not to be ministered unto, but to minister, and to give his life a ransom for many" (Matthew 20:28). As Jesus did, we must live a sacrificial life since God rewards sacrifice. Intercessors offer their lives by praying for others to get comfort and joy. The Apostles likewise surrendered their activities to preach the gospel. So, we must submit and pray for others' good, as shown by Jesus Christ. The primary mandate of intercessors in the Kingdom of God is to love and help others and pray for them.

> [1] *"So I beseech you therefore, brethren, by the mercies of God, that ye present your bodies a living sacrifice, holy, acceptable unto God, which is your reasonable service," — **Romans 12:1***

Honesty

Scriptures demand that Christian life be marked with integrity and honesty, but sin leads to deceit. Honesty is being truthful. It is being free from deceit or untruthfulness. Honesty is the basis for trust in a relationship. However, it does not mean that you should tell everything you know, even when it means that it can harm someone.

Honest people are sincere in their dealings with others. They are true to their words and actions. The person who tells the truth is free from evil. Thus, honesty makes us free from those who accuse us. Therefore, we must not exaggerate, defraud, gossip, or backbite others. Instead, we must preach the truth and practice the same. Our words must be truthfully transparent, admitting wrongs and showing empathy for others.

- Honesty pleases God. Therefore, we must walk in truthfulness and faithfulness as children of the light. The Bible says, "Lying lips are detestable to the Lord, but faithful people are His delight" (Proverbs 12:22). So. the truth must be told with an open heart, even in challenging circumstances. We must keep the promises we make to God and other people.

Honesty was an outstanding quality of Christ's life. He was honest in all His dealings with man. Jesus never lied nor defrauded anybody. He chastised the Jewish leaders for misleading and defrauding the people. For instance, He rebuked the covetous Pharisees for cheating widows and those selling in the house of God. Jesus taught us honesty and a good heart in keeping God's laws. Zacchaeus was a wealthy tax collector who was dishonest in keeping some tax money. When he met Jesus, he pledged to give half of his possessions to the poor and repay those he had cheated. A dishonest Zacchaeus became honest when he had an encounter with Jesus.

On the contrary, Ananias and Sapphira lied to Peter the Apostle when they kept a portion of the money from the land they sold, but told everyone that they had given the total sum. Peter then confronted Ananias' deceit, and they were mortally punished. God hates and judges' dishonesty. He values honesty in words and action, not deception since He cannot lie (Titus 1:2). As believers in Christ, we must be honest no matter where we find ourselves at home, at work, at school, and in all relationships. We cannot get away with dishonesty because He judges it.

> *"But let your communication be, Yea, yea; Nay, nay: for whatsoever is more than these cometh of evil." — **Matthew 5:37.***

Truth is God's very nature. Jesus Christ is the way, the truth, and the life. With Jesus as our example, believers are called to value truthfulness and honesty. God made honesty a commandment because He cannot lie. He sets the standard for His people.

> *"Finally, brethren, whatsoever things are true, whatsoever things are honest, whatsoever things are just, whatsoever things are pure, whatsoever things are lovely, whatsoever things are of good report; if there be any virtue, and if there be any praise, think on these things." — **Philippians 4:8-9***

We must choose not to steal, cheat, or deceive, but to build honest character to serve God and man. We are to emulate Jesus' truthfulness since God will trust us and answer our prayers.

Humility

Jesus is humble and meek. He is our model of humility. Although He is one with the Father and shares eternal glory with Him, Jesus surrendered to God's will. Besides, He never sought the praise of men for all the wonderful works God did through Him. Jesus is the son of the almighty God, yet He did not boast of His divinity.

> "*⁶Who, being in the form of God, thought it not robbery to be equal with God. ⁷But made himself of no reputation, and took upon him the form of a servant, and was made in the likeness of men:⁸ And being found in fashion as a man, he humbled himself, and became obedient unto death, even the death of the cross."* — **Philippians 2:6-8.**

The Lord Jesus was born in a lowly manger to His earthly parents, a virgin, and a carpenter. As a child, He grew up in the despised city of Nazareth. He humbly submitted to His earthly parents throughout His youth. John baptized the sinless Son of God in the Jordan. Christ showed humility during His earthly ministry as He associated with the lowly regarded, including Samaritans, sinners, Gentiles, the poor, tax collectors, and the oppressed.

Jesus also demonstrated servant leadership. He humbly washed the Apostles' feet, a task usually performed by servants. He brought the kingdom of God and its dominion to man, which included righteousness, peace, and joy. To save the lost, He preached the gospel and set the oppressed free from a sinful and destructive lifestyle. Also, He healed the sick and raised the dead. For example, Jesus restored the life of the Samaritan woman at the well when he offered her divine mercy. The Jews had low regard for the Samaritans, but Jesus ignored the Jewish superiority and approached her, resulting in the salvation of an entire community (John 4:39-42).

He never demanded praise for His miracles and teachings, even when the people sought to make Him king. Instead, Jesus gave all the honor to God. Jesus showed humility in all His endeavors, despite being God by nature. Faced with the agony of a shameful death, Jesus prayed and submitted to the Father, "Saying, Father, if thou be willing, remove this cup from me: nevertheless, not my will, but thine, be done" (Luke 22:42). Thus, He died the most painful and shameful death devised by immoral men.

However, Jesus spoke against those who craved the praises of men (Matthew 6:1-6). He condemned man's inclination towards amassing wealth, tradition, legalism, exploiting the poor by the rich, and the maltreatment of orphans and widows. He also criticized the authoritarian leadership style of the Pharisees and the Jewish leaders, who loved to be praised and served by the people. Our effort to accomplish anything without God will be fruitless, since all power and wisdom belong to Him. Every one of us has a purpose, and we utterly depend on God by putting our faith in Him. Intercessors approach God in humility, sincerity, reverence, and awe. Those who attract God's blessing are humble, obedient, and faithful.

We must humbly intercede for others without self-righteousness and condemnation. Humility means acknowledging that our righteousness and abilities are gifts from God. A humble heart also acknowledges human weaknesses and genuinely rejoices when others prosper and triumph. It overlooks pettiness and easily forgives others. Therefore, humility allows you to let go of control and take the backstage to help others (1 Peter 5:5).

84

Compassion

Christ impeccably reflected God's compassion for humanity. Jesus had sympathy not just for Israel, but for the whole of humanity because of God's love. He was the love of God in action during His earthly ministry. He had compassion for sinners and the afflicted. Therefore, we must show compassion to the people we pray for (John 3:16). When Jesus saw the distressed multitude scattered abroad like a shepherdless flock, He taught them the word and healed them (Mark 6:34).

As Jesus walked through towns and villages, He was not only concerned about the spiritual misery of men, but He also ministered to their physical needs. He fed the hungry multitude (Mark 8:2; Matthew 14:14). His disciples also showed a lot of compassion for the helpless.

Peter prayed and healed the man at the beautiful gate in the name of Jesus. Paul wept at the very thought of Christians living in sin, through the deceit of false teachers (Acts 20:18-38).

> *"Be kind and compassionate to one another, forgiving each, just as in Christ God forgave you." — **Ephesians 4:32.***

> *Finally, be ye all of one mind, having compassion one of another, love as brethren, be pitiful, be courteous:* — ***Ephesians 4:32.***

***

God wants intercessors to be passionately compassionate, like Jesus, for the hurting and weary through prayer and deeds. People's infirmities and challenges must touch us to pray for them.

Fruits of the Holy Spirit

Before His ascension, Jesus promised His disciples another helper, the Holy Spirit, to be their comforter, teacher, and guide. The Holy Spirit possesses the same godly traits as Jesus (John 16:13-15). He also convicts the world of sin, righteousness, and judgment. Christ empowers believers with the Holy Spirit. Paul urged believers to bear the fruit of the spirit (Galatians 5:22-23) and avoid fleshly works. Intercessors bear the fruit of the spirit (John 14) for effective intercession.

> *"²²But the fruit of the Spirit is love, joy, peace, longsuffering, gentleness, goodness, faith, ²³Meekness, temperance: against such there is no law. ²⁴And they that are Christ's have crucified the flesh with the affections and lusts." — **Galatians 5:22-24***

Love

Love is self-sacrifice, putting others' needs before ours, and humbly following Jesus' servanthood example (Phil. 2). It is an essential trait of the believer and evidence of the presence of the Holy Spirit in our hearts. God showed His perfect, selfless, agape love to the world through Jesus when He sent Him to die for our sins. Therefore, God commands us to love one another. Love is the greatest gift from God.

> *"Love is patient, love is kind. It is not jealous, is not pompous, it is not inflated, it is not rude, it does not seek its own interests, it is not quick-tempered, it does not brood over injury, it does not rejoice over wrongdoing but rejoices with the truth. It bears all things, believes all things, hopes all things, endures all things." — **1 Corinthians 13:4-7***

We cannot love ideally without the help of the Holy Spirit. He helps us to put away our sinfulness and selfishness. The Holy Spirit teaches us the love of God through Christ and then helps us to love God and others in obedience and service. We show love for others through self-sacrifice in words and actions (1 John 4:19-21). Jesus' parable of the Good Samaritan teaches us to love everyone, including our enemies. It is naturally easy to love friends and family, but it takes the help of the Holy Spirit to love those who harm or hurt us. We should put aside our differences and help those who need help. The Samaritans saw a man who needed help and ignored the hostility between Jews and Samaritans. We must help all men with our talent and gifts for God's glory (Luke 10:25-37). God's love is for all humanity (John 3:16).

Absolute Joy

Joy is not based on a momentary physical circumstance, but on faith in the unfailing love of God, no matter the situation. Joy follows love and relates to supreme hope or the absolute assurance of future glory in Jesus Christ.

Jesus was joyful and prayed that His disciples might have such joy (John 17:13). People in the Bible who obeyed God had joy despite their circumstances. Joy is the immediate benefit of obedience. A notable example is when Paul and Silas were beaten and jailed because they delivered a demon-possessed girl. They did not complain. Instead, they sang and praised God in their affliction, and God responded with a mighty deliverance. In addition, they spread the good news and helped others.

> *"May the God of hope fill you with all joy and peace as you trust in him, so that you may overflow with hope by the power of the Holy Spirit." — **Romans 15:13***

87

Paul and Silas had a choice to complain or rejoice in the Lord, and they praised God in their afflictions. No matter what happens, we should turn to God and praise Him for everything. We can find joy in challenging situations because the Holy Spirit is our comforter. God calls us to rejoice always and live a life full of joy.

Peace

Peace is harmony in the heart and with others. We can only have peace in Christ as we submit to His will (Philippians 4:6-7, Isaiah 26:3). God's presence produces peace, purpose, and power in every moment of our lives. Peace helps us maintain a loving relationship with God and others and grants us the ability to accomplish God's desire in our lives. Conversely, spiteful relationships adversely affect our communion with God. Therefore, we must be at peace with everybody.

> *"11 Follow peace with all men, and holiness, without which no man shall see the Lord:" — **Hebrews 12:14***

Jesus was at peace with all men. Similarly, the Holy Spirit does not operate where there is confusion, for God has set the order of command in every relationship. Jesus taught us to reconcile with our offended relations before presenting our offerings and prayers to the Lord. He also admonished us to settle disputes with opponents quickly, even when they cheat us (Matthew 5:23-25; 39-41). Jesus died and reconciled sinful man with God, though humanity did not deserve this great sacrifice. Likewise, Jesus has given believers the ministry of reconciliation to preach the good news to the lost. Intercessors must always be peacemakers. When we surrender every situation to the Lord in prayer, He gives us His peace beyond human comprehension.

Longsuffering

Long-suffering is enduring patience in the face of challenges. It is self-restraint or not giving way to anger when faced with provocation. Patience follows peace and exhibits tolerance and resilience towards challenging circumstances.

Jesus patiently waited amid tribulations and fulfilled His mandate on the cross. He rejected the ungodly shortcuts Satan offered Him. Similarly, intercessors must be patient with God and man. We must wait for God's timing to accomplish His purpose for us. We must patiently wait for answers to prayers without seeking human and ungodly solutions, even in the face of challenges.

Also, intercessors must be patient with the people they intercede for without condemnation. Jesus had patience with all those who came to Him for help. Even the Pharisees and scribes who intentionally tempted Him with questions hoping to trap Him, Jesus patiently answered them. The Word of God tells us to wait patiently for the Lord. Impatience, annoyance, intolerance, and worry prevent us from pleasing God.

> *"Now we exhort you, brethren, warn them that are unruly, comfort the feebleminded, support the weak, be patient toward all men." — 1 Thessalonians 5:14*

As Paul and Silas did in jail, God wants us to be patient in all situations so that He can give us victory (Acts 16:25; Romans 8:28). Patience strengthens us to forgive and manage anger. We must persevere in prayer despite obstacles or delays to answers. Therefore, intercessors must avoid frustrations, irritability, and bitterness as we intercede for others (Matthew 22:35-40).

Kindness

Kindness is acting for people's good regardless of what they do and expecting no rewards. It is a genuine concern for others in words and deeds. Kindness involves caring for and sharing our gifts with others. God daily shows His Kindness to humanity. Apart from salvation, He provides the needs of every living thing. Besides, the Holy Spirit helps us bear this quality as we acknowledge that God wants us to share our blessings with others (Matthew 5:43-45; Romans 11:22; Ephesians 2:7; Titus 3:4-6).

> *"I have shewed you all things, how that so labouring ye ought to support the weak, and to remember the words of the Lord Jesus, how he said, It is more blessed to give than to receive."* — *Acts 20:35*

> *"And be ye kind one to another, tenderhearted, forgiving one another, even as God for Christ's sake hath forgiven you."* — *Ephesians 4:32*

Jesus showed kindness to all the people that came to Him. He empathized with their sufferings and provided for them. Jesus never condemned sinners. Instead, He preached the gospel to them, healed the sick, delivered the oppressed, and miraculously provided food for them. Thus, we show kindness when we share what we have with others and care for their well-being.

Kindness touches hearts and uniquely connects people. People are more likely to receive our message when we show them kindness. We can show others kindness by empathizing with their challenges and providing for their needs, praying for them, and being considerate in words and actions.

Gentleness

Gentleness means being tender in actions and words. Jesus had a gentle disposition throughout His earthly ministry. He never treated or talked harshly to anyone, including the Pharisees and His accusers. When they questioned Him about His works and authority, He gently answered them, though He perceived their evil intentions.

> *"¹⁷That it might be fulfilled which was spoken by Esaias the prophet, saying, ¹⁸Behold my servant, whom I have chosen; my beloved, in whom my soul is well pleased: I will put my spirit upon him, and he shall shew judgment to the Gentiles. ¹⁹He shall not strive, nor cry; neither shall any man hear his voice in the streets. ²⁰A bruised reed shall he not break, and smoking flax shall he not quench, till he send forth judgment unto victory."* — **Matthew 12:17-20**

> *"And the servant of the Lord must not strive; but be gentle unto all men, apt to teach, patient,"* — **2 Timothy 2:24**

> *"Let no corrupt communication proceed out of your mouth, but that which is good to the use of edifying, that it may minister grace unto the hearers."* — **Ephesians 4:29**

Jesus' gentleness also showed in how He treated people who came to Him for help. He did not abuse anyone in words or actions. Instead, He was gentle to all, including sinners. As a result, the people gladly received Jesus because He was considerate and affectionate, unlike the Pharisees, who defrauded and maltreated them. Therefore, intercessors must be gentle and not treat harshly people who are in need.

Goodness

Being good, moral excellence; virtue, kindness; generosity, excellence of quality, goodness of workmanship.

Jesus showed goodness throughout His earthly ministry. He was good to everyone, including those who tortured and crucified Him. There was no wickedness in Him; neither did He connive evil. Jesus genuinely cared for the people He ministered to. God is good to us every day, though we do not deserve His goodness because of our sins. We must also show goodness from our hearts to others.

> *"How God anointed Jesus of Nazareth with the Holy Ghost and with power: who went about doing good, and healing all that were oppressed of the devil; for God was with him."* — *Acts 10:38*

Goodness also means we should also correct wrongdoings in love. We must not condone wickedness. For instance, Jesus was good to the woman caught in adultery, but He did not overlook her sin. He did not condemn her, but He counseled her to live uprightly.

> *"⁸For ye were sometimes darkness, but now are ye light in the Lord: walk as children of light: ⁹(For the fruit of the Spirit is in all goodness and righteousness and truth;) ¹⁰Proving what is acceptable unto the Lord."* — *Ephesians 5:8-10*

Faith

Faith is believing in the love and goodness of God. It is the basis of our obedience to Him. God's word is the only source of faith. Our faith grows as we focus our hearts and attention on what He has already accomplished. Intercessors can break strongholds by displacing anxiety or fear and nurturing unshakable faith. Faith is confidence in God through Jesus Christ. His dedication to the truth and triumphant life gives us the strength to overcome the world. Faith comes from trusting the loving father that we have in God. We activate our faith when we believe in God's greatness and love and are confident of His will and purpose. Therefore, intercessors must have faith in God's love to answer our prayers as we stand in the gap for others.

> *"So then faith cometh by hearing, and hearing by the word of God." — **Romans 10:17***

Faith is necessary to please God because He wants us to believe He exists and rewards those who seek Him (Hebrews 11:6). Faith is confidence in the grace and mercy of God. For example, Jesus had faith in the Father's love for Him. He also believed God always heard His supplications. Similarly, people who expressed their faith in Jesus received healing. For instance, Jesus praised the Roman centurion's faith as an example for the Jews and the Galileans, who had a more significant opportunity to receive His blessings. Jesus also commended the faith of the Canaanite woman who asked for deliverance for her demon-possessed daughter.

As the Holy Spirit leads intercessors, they have faith in God for solutions in challenging situations. Thus, the Apostles did many miracles because they believed in God through Jesus. Jesus said we can perform greater works than He did if only we believe (John 14:12).

Faith in Jesus leads to trust in our service to God and a firm commitment to others. God is faithful because He keeps His promises and covenants. No matter what humans do, God keeps His promises. For example, God promised to send His son to redeem humanity, fulfilling it at the appropriate time when Jesus died for our sins. Likewise, Jesus was faithful in all His deeds and words. He faithfully executed God's redemption plan for man. He was also faithful in His dealings with the people so no one could accuse Him of wrongdoing. Jesus taught His disciples to be faithful by comparing the Kingdom of God to faithfulness in stewardship (Matthew 25:14-30). Similarly, intercessors must be faithful to the mandate to stand in the gap for others.

> *"Wherefore, holy brethren, partakers of the heavenly calling, consider the Apostle and High Priest of our profession, Christ Jesus; [2]Who was faithful to him that appointed him, as also Moses was faithful in all his house." — **Hebrews 3:1-2**

> *"Let a man so account of us, as of the ministers of Christ, and stewards of the mysteries of God. [2]Moreover it is required in stewards, that a man be found faithful." — **1 Corinth. 4:1-2**

As a faithful God, He stands by His people in difficult times. Satan cannot tempt God's children beyond their ability to resist, and God always provides an escape route. As God's children, we have confidence in the future not because we are faithful, but because He is faithful to His promise of eternal life. When we confess our sins, we believe God forgives us because He is righteous and faithful to His word. Doubting whether God has forgiven you when you repent is questioning His faithfulness. Therefore, we must believe in God's faithfulness to answer our prayers.

Meekness

Meekness is the humbleness and gentleness of the heart. A meek person acknowledges God as the source of every good thing, so he does not boast but accepts corrections. As a child, Jesus humbly submitted to the guidance of His earthly parents, though He was the son of God. He left His heavenly glory to come to this sinful world to die for humanity. Jesus did not complain when He was abused because He willingly surrendered to the will of the Father. They took Him to the cross like a sheep to slaughter, though He could have defended Himself. Jesus was meek but did not deny His identity as the Messiah. However, He did not boast about the mighty works God did through Him. Instead, He warned those He healed and delivered not to broadcast miracles.

"Blessed are the meek: for they shall inherit the earth." — *Matthew 5:5*

"Take my yoke upon you, and learn of me; for I am meek and lowly in heart: and ye shall find rest unto your souls." — *Matthew 11:29*

"Tell ye the daughter of Sion, Behold, thy King cometh unto thee, meek, and sitting upon an ass, and a colt the foal of an ass." — *Matthew 21-5*

Intercessors must be meek. Like Jesus, we should use our God-given gifts to assist others, not demean or take advantage of them, demonstrating our ultimate humility. Intercessors must acknowledge and honor God as the giver of everything. Jesus never took God's glory. So, intercessors must not take credit for answered prayers because we can do nothing without Him. Without the help of the Holy

Spirit, we can do worse things than the sinners we condemn. Thus, intercessors should not behave like the Pharisees who arrogantly trusted their righteousness and judged sinners.

Temperance

Temperance means self-control or discipline. The Holy Spirit helps us to control our desires for worldly things. Jesus always had self-control and did not indulge in anything that would not glorify His Father. When the devil tempted Him after a forty-day fast, Jesus immediately rejected the devil's ungodly offers using the scriptures. He had control over His desires.

> *"And when the tempter came to him, he said, If thou be the Son of God, command that these stones be made bread. But he answered and said, It is written, Man shall not live by bread alone, but by every word that proceedeth out of the mouth of God." — Matthew 4:3-4*

Jesus lived a modest life on earth, though God had given everything to Him. He said anyone who lustily desires worldly things cannot sincerely serve God. For instance, Jesus warned we cannot serve God and money. Thus, intercessors must avoid greed and the lure of this world. Similarly, we must control our desires and not be easily influenced by situations around us.

> *"15Love not the world, neither the things that are in the world. If any man love the world, the love of the Father is not in him. 16For all that is in the world, the lust of the flesh, and the lust of the eyes, and the pride of life, is not of the Father, but is of the world." — 1 John 2:15-16*

Qualities of intercessors in the New Testament

Prayer was a priority to the early Christians who continued Jesus' ministry of intercession. They emulated Jesus' qualities, such as faith, obedience, humility, patience, and perseverance. Intercessors abide by God's Word to attain the desired blessing. Jesus knew that without the power from heaven, the disciples would fail. So, He told them to wait in Jerusalem for empowerment. Thus, as Jesus promised, the Holy Spirit empowered them with boldness and unction (Acts 1:13-14; 2:1-4). They prayed with unity and in harmony with the Word of God (Acts 4:23-31). As a result, the Apostles were earnest in ministry (James 5:17).

The Apostles had great faith in God through Jesus. In the name of Jesus, they interceded for healing and deliverance from unclean spirits (Act 2-9; 3:15:16). Also, the Apostles were humble and gave glory to God for the wonderful works done through them. They never took credit for the power of God to heal and deliver. They were gentle and treated the people with kindness. Worldly things did not lure them from their godly mandate. They had compassion for the lost and did not defraud the people.

Prayer is a potent weapon God has given His children to fulfill the mission He has entrusted to us. The Apostles were persistent in the face of severe threats from the Pharisees. As Jesus told them, the Apostles suffered beatings, imprisonment, and death, but they persevered in the ministry. Thus, intercessors must persist, even in challenging situations.

Intercessors are vessels of honor who must exhibit godly traits. God always sets the standard for His servants, since none can approach the Holy God with uncleanliness. As a result, He consecrates and anoints men to honor Him. He also desires a humble heart, obedience, and faithfulness in worship. The Levitical priests had godly characteristics, though they exhibited flaws. But the ultimate intercessor, Jesus, was the only perfect intercessor. He is also the sinless vessel who defeated Satan. Love, peace, compassion, patience, and obedience were qualities He exhibited in His earthly ministry. He has empowered every believer with the Spirit to live a holy life and bear spiritual fruits.

The next chapter, the principles of intercession, details how God's presence has become accessible to man because Jesus fulfilled the law on our behalf and empowered every believer with His righteousness. He also gave us a perfect prayer and intercession model.

4

Principles of Intercession

How do intercessors present effective prayers on behalf of others? God always provided a prayer model of how His people should appear before Him in prayers. In the Old Testament, His people worshipped and prayed by offering animal sacrifices on altars to Him (Genesis 4:3). When God appointed the Levitical priests in Israel, He directed them on how to appear before Him with sacrifices and offerings for Israel. Only the high priest ministered before Him in the Holy place, sprinkling animal blood on the Mercy Seat to atone for sins committed by the Israelites on the Day of Atonement, and made intercession. Yet there was a yearly reminder of sin, for the animal blood could not eradicate sin.

But, in the New Testament, God sent His only Son, Jesus, who offered Himself as a sacrifice. He performed the ultimate atonement for humanity with His blood. He cleansed Himself and humanity once with His blood, obliviating the need for animal sacrifices and burnt offerings before prayers (Hebrews. 10). He tore the veil of the Temple, and in allegoric significance, God's presence became accessible to all humanity. Thus, Jesus not only fulfilled the law on our behalf, but also blessed us with a New Testament purified and sealed with His blood. God appointed Jesus as our High Priest, who, in turn, has empowered us as Godly priests with His righteousness. He also gave us a perfect prayer and intercession model.

Model for Standing in the Gap in the Old Testament

The Bible does not state when God first requested sacrifices and offerings on altars as worship and prayer, but Cain and Abel gave animals and fruit of the ground as offerings to the Lord (Genesis 4:3-5). Noah built an altar and offered burned sacrifices after the flood. Similarly, when God promised to give Canaan to his descendants, Abraham built an altar to the Lord. Likewise, after being commanded by God, Jacob complied and constructed an altar in Bethel, where he dwelled as well (Genesis 8:20-22; 12:1-8, 35:1-7).

Later, God institutionalized a prayer model for Moses and the Levitical priesthood after the Israelites left Egypt. First, God commanded Moses to build the tabernacle of the congregation, a portable place of worship, according to the pattern He showed him on Mount Sinai. Second, only the priests could offer animal sacrifices and burned offerings for Israel before Him in the tabernacle. Among other priestly duties, He instructed them to offer daily and seasonal animal sacrifices and offerings on the altar for Israel. Also, the priests cleansed themselves and wore holy clothes before rendering service in the tabernacle. Thus, God required the priests to be holy. He commanded Israel to observe **the day of atonement** on the tenth day of the seventh month as follows (Leviticus 16).:

- A Sabbath with fasting for Israel.
- The **High Priest**, the only person permitted to enter the **Holy of Holies**, made it right with God by offering a ram sacrifice to cleanse himself and his household of sin.
- He brought a **burning incense** before the Lord, and the cloud of incense covered the mercy seat above the testimony to prevent death when he entered the Holy Place.

- The high priest passed through the veil and entered this sacred dwelling once a year. God cannot look on or tolerate sin, so the veil was a barrier between man and the holy God.
- The high priest offered sacrifices for himself, his household, and Israel's uncleanness and rebellion.
- **For the atonement**, they brought two goats for a sin offering and a ram for a burned offering.
- The high priest sprinkles the blood (one goat and one ram) on the Mercy Seat to atone for Israel's sins and cleanses the Holy Place, the altar, and the Tent of Meeting (Leviticus 16).
- The high priest puts his hands on the head of the live goat and confesses Israel's sins, and the goat shall bear their sins. Then they send the scapegoat to an uninhabited land.
- They burned the fat of the animals on the brazen altar.
- The priests then blessed the people.

However, some Levitical priests failed this noble mandate and led Israel astray. Consequently, God honored those who obeyed His Word. He chose Judah and established His promise with David's lineage, making Jerusalem the place of worship where Solomon built the Temple.

Judah also committed harlotry and other pagan practices. They blended the worship of God with the idolatry of Molech, Baal, and other foreign gods to defile the Temple. They despised the holy vessels and desecrated the Sabbaths. They also abandoned the law until King Josiah removed the worship of Baal, Asherah, Tophet, and other gods from the Temple and killed the Baal priests. God also anointed priests like Isaiah and Jeremiah in Judah to intercede for Israel.

Yet, continued disobedience and idolatry defiled Judah. Thus, God rejected Judah, and His presence departed from the Temple in Jerusalem because they committed harlotry. He delivered Judah into the hands of their spoilers; they became victims of the Babylonian raid. King Nebuchadnezzar took the Holy vessels and destroyed the Temple. Judah went into exile for 70 years.

After the Temple's destruction, and Israel's dispersal, they petitioned God without animal sacrifices. Instead, they confessed their sins and acknowledged God's mercy before presenting their prayers. Fasting was also a central part of intercession. Nevertheless, God preserved a remnant of Judah because of His covenant with David. Prophets like Daniel interceded for Judah in Babylon without animal sacrifices.

> *"8 Yet will I leave a remnant, that ye may have some that shall escape the sword among the nations, when ye shall be scattered through the countries." — **Ezekiel 6:8***

Judah later returned to Jerusalem, rebuilt the temple, and resumed the service in the Temple. The priests' role in the Temple continued until Jesus offered the ultimate intercession for the sins of humanity — fulfilling God's covenants with Abraham and David (Genesis 4-18)

> *"16 In those days shall Judah be saved, and Jerusalem shall dwell safely: and this is the name wherewith she shall be called, The Lord our righteousness. For thus saith the Lord; David shall never want a man to sit upon the throne of the house of Israel;18 Neither shall the priests the Levites want a man before me to offer burnt offerings, and to kindle meat offerings, and to do sacrifice continually." — **Jer. 33:14-18***

Model of Intercession in the New Testament

John the Baptist prepares the way for Jesus

John was the bridge between the Old and the New Testaments as God anointed him with the Holy Spirit to prepare the way for the Messiah. John came in the spirit and power of Elijah, the prophet, to turn the children of Israel to the Lord and prepare their hearts to receive the gospel. Before the ministry of Jesus, John preached repentance and baptism to all the people of Israel. He also baptized Jesus and introduced Him to the people as God's Anointed One. He testified about Jesus, saying:

> *"[15]saying, This was he of whom I spake, He that cometh after me is preferred before me: for he was before me. [16]And of his fulness have all we received, and grace for grace. [17]For the law was given by Moses, but grace and truth came by Jesus Christ." — John 1:15-16*

How Jesus interceded

Jesus interceded for people according to the commandment of God. He expressed gratitude to the Father for always listening to Him always. Because God has given Him all power, Jesus healed and delivered the people as He preached the gospel of the Kingdom of God. He fulfilled the requirements for us when He cleansed our sins with His precious blood as our sacrificial lamb. He has given us a new covenant in His blood; thus, we are no longer required to fulfill the law of animal sacrifice. As our eternal high priest, Jesus sits at the right hand of God, interceding for us. Jesus Christ showed us a new way to worship and pray to God. He told the Samaritan woman that God now wants us to worship Him in spirit and truth, and not in Jerusalem or Mount Sinai (John 4:21-26).

Jesus, the only way to God

Under the New Testament, Jesus is the only way to God (John 14:6). As our eternal high priest, we pray in His name to the Father. He is the only mediator between God and man.

> [6] *Jesus saith unto him, I am the way, the truth, and the life: no man cometh unto the Father, but by me.* —- *John 14:6*

God has entrusted everything to Jesus and given Him a name that everything submits to. The Apostles interceded in the name of Jesus. In Him, we have victory. Therefore, intercessors pray to God only in the name of Jesus. We receive salvation, deliverance, and all the benefits of the New Testament in the name of Jesus. We can do nothing without Him (John 15). Jesus also gave us a prayer model comprising:

- **Privacy** — Pray to the Father in secret.
- **Adoration-** "Our Father which art in heaven."
- **God's Will** — "Thy kingdom come;"
- **Daily Needs** — "Give us this day our daily bread."
- **Pardon** — "Forgive us our sins as we forgive others."
- **Petition** — "Deliverance from temptation and evil."
- **Thanksgiving** — "For thine is the kingdom."
- **Fasting**
- **Perseverance**
- **Always and at Midnight** (Matthew 6:5-18).

Privacy

Jesus openly prayed for people to receive their deliverance, but He also had unique places where He retreated for prayer. For example, He often woke up early morning and went alone to a solitary place or the mountainside to commune with God (Mark 1:34-35). He also withdrew himself into the wilderness, and prayed after ministering to the people.

He took Peter, John, and James, and went up on a mountain to pray. As He was praying, the appearance of His face changed, and His clothes became radiantly white. Jesus also advised us to pray secretly, so God will reward us openly.

> *"And when thou prayest, thou shalt not be as the hypocrites are: for they love to pray, standing in the synagogues and in the corners of the streets, that they may be seen of men. Verily I say unto you, They have their reward. 6 But thou, when thou prayest, enter into thy closet, and when thou hast shut thy door, pray to thy Father which is in secret; and thy Father which seeth in secret shall reward thee openly." — **Matthew 6:5, 6**

Although the Apostles ministered to the people openly, they usually gathered indoors to pray. Intercessory prayer sessions involve shutting out all interferences and interruptions, forbidding open display, and placing all thoughts upon God alone to take a complete inventory of us and intervene for others. A private prayer life increases our fellowship with God. God cherishes a personal relationship as joy comes with our fellowship with Him.

Adoration

Adoration is an intense admiration in reverence and attitude in worship before the Lord, our Maker. Jesus always adored the Father. He also taught the disciples to start their prayers with worship by worshiping the heavenly Father. We adore God by declaring His divine nature and sanctifying His name with words and songs. The heavenly hosts worship God by prostrating and proclaiming His glory, power, and honor (Revelation 4). In worship, some people kneel while others prostrate before the Lord. But no matter your posture, the important thing is your adoration must come from your heart. Jesus said God wants us to worship Him in spirit and truth (John 4). Therefore, we must come before God with adoration from a pure and loving heart. We worship God because we love Him for who He is.

> *"Our Father which art in heaven, Hallowed be thy name.[10] Thy kingdom come, Thy will be done in earth, as it is in heaven." — **Matthew 6:9-10***

> *"8And the four beasts had each of them six wings about him, and they were full of eyes within: and they rest not day and night, saying, Holy, holy, holy, Lord God Almighty, which was, and is, and is to come. 9And when those beasts give glory and honour and thanks to him that sat on the throne, who liveth for ever and ever, 10 The four and twenty elders fall down before him that sat on the throne, and worship him that liveth for ever and ever, and cast their crowns before the throne, saying, 11Thou art worthy, O Lord, to receive glory and honour and power: for thou hast created all things, and for thy pleasure they are and were created." — **Revelation 4:8-11***

God wants His children to adore Him. So when the Pharisees questioned Jesus why the people were praising God during His triumphant entry into Jerusalem, He said the stones would cry out if they kept quiet.

> *"⁴⁰And he answered and said unto them, I tell you that, if these should hold their peace, the stones would immediately cry out." — **Luke 19:37-40***

Thus, we humbly approach God as the Sovereign Lord, who made Heaven and Earth, genuinely recognizing His holiness, greatness, righteousness, and perfection in everything. In worship, we testify God is greater than all and worthy of our adoration. God desires and deserves sincere worship. Then we continue with praise, joyfully recounting all God's good and mighty works. With gratitude in our hearts, we appreciate God's righteous deeds. We praise Him for His goodness and mercy. Jesus always praised and thanked God for His love for humanity. Praise and worship draw God's presence. For instance, when Paul and Silas praised and worshipped God in jail, His presence shook the entire building, and there was a mighty deliverance because there is freedom in His presence. Similarly, God's presence filled the place where the disciples were worshipping Him after the Pharisees threatened them not to heal or preach in the name of Jesus.

As we praise and worship God, His presence overshadows us and sets us free from bondage, especially from the spirit of heaviness. Then He fills us with the spirit of joy. Thus, praise and worship are critical in intercession. We must praise and worship Him in every situation and everywhere with songs and loving words. However, we can only adore God if we know who He is by studying and obeying His word.

God's Will

Jesus executed the will of the Father in His early ministry. He emulated whatever God did. Our heavenly Father answers prayers according to His will. Thus, Jesus' actions, speech, and intercessions conformed to God's will.

For instance, He submitted to God's will when He agonized in the garden of Gethsemane because He knew God would surely choose the redemption plan for humanity over His temporary suffering. God gave authority and power to Jesus to accomplish His will on earth. He has also anointed and empowered believers through Jesus with the Holy Spirit to continue His will on earth.

> *"[19]Then answered Jesus and said unto them, Verily, verily, I say unto you, The Son can do nothing of himself, but what he seeth the Father do: for what things soever he doeth, these also doeth the Son likewise. [20]For the Father loveth the Son, and sheweth him all things that himself doeth: and he will shew him greater works than these, that ye may marvel. [21]For as the Father raiseth up the dead, and quickeneth them; even so the Son quickeneth whom he will." — **John 5:19-21***

How do intercessors know the will of God?

We can only know the mind of God in every situation through His word - the Bible and revelation. The Holy Spirit speaks to us through the Word of God. Moreover, the Spirit takes the doctrines of Christ, the Word of God, and simplifies them for the believer. He does not act independently of the Word of God. Thus, the believer led by the Spirit is a doer of the Word (John 16:13-15).

"¹²I have yet many things to say unto you, but ye cannot bear them now. ¹³Howbeit when he, the Spirit of truth, is come, he will guide you into all truth: for he shall not speak of himself; but whatsoever he shall hear, that shall he speak: and he will shew you things to come. ¹⁴He shall glorify me: for he shall receive of mine, and shall shew it unto you." — **John 16:13-14**

The Holy Spirit, our teacher, helps us to understand God's word to know what He desires from us. God answers prayers according to His will, as documented in His Word. He will not answer our prayers if we ask for anything beyond His promises. God will not grant us everything we ask from Him because He knows what is best for us. For effective prayer, we must learn what God has promised in His word through reading the Bible. Then we can base our prayers on them. We pray for God's promises by proclaiming His word. Further, without the guidance of the Holy Spirit, we would live in carnality, governed by the old sinful nature, rebellion, and out of fellowship with God. The Holy Spirit helps believers to live a Christ-like character and enables them to execute God's plan.

Additionally, God has empowered believers with spiritual gifts to know His will in real-time. They include wisdom, knowledge, faith, healing, miracles, prophecy, discernment, tongues, and interpretation of tongues. The gift of healing is the manifestation of the Spirit of God that miraculously brings healing and deliverance. There are other gifts, such as dreams and visions. Jesus said the Holy Spirit would show us revelations of things God has freely given us.

Every believer must know how the Holy Spirit communicates to him. The Apostles used these gifts in their intercession as they preached the gospel. They healed the sick and released the oppressed to the glory of God. For instance, Peter, empowered with the gift of healing, prayed for the healing of the lame at the Beautiful Gate of the temple (Acts 3:2). Likewise, Paul witnessed signs and wonders in many places He preached the gospel. Like the Apostles, we must use these gifts to release people from the devil's oppression. However, God will chastise us if we use these freely given gifts of the Spirit for selfish gains.

> *"But the manifestation of the Spirit is given to every man to profit withal. ⁸For to one is given by the Spirit the word of wisdom; to another the word of knowledge by the same Spirit; ⁹To another faith by the same Spirit; to another the gifts of healing by the same Spirit; ¹⁰To another the working of miracles; to another prophecy; to another discerning of spirits; to another divers kinds of tongues; to another the interpretation of tongues: ¹¹But all these worketh that one and the selfsame Spirit, dividing to every man severally as he will."* — **1 Corinthians 12:7-11**

Our natural senses cannot perceive matters of the spirit. Therefore, intercessors must be sensitive to the Holy Spirit, especially during prayers. For instance, God told Ananias in a vision to pray for Paul, who had become blind after an encounter with the Lord for persecuting the church. Paul also received a vision about Ananias coming to help him (Acts 9:10-20). Also, Paul was directed in a night vision to go to Macedonia and help. We must not be complacent, but rely on the leading of the Spirit. For instance, the Holy Spirit stopped Paul from preaching the gospel in Asia. Instead, he was directed in a night vision to go to Macedonia and help (Acts 16:6-10).

Pardon - forgiveness of trespasses

God cannot tolerate sin. Our sins must be washed through the satisfied sacrificial demands required by the Holy God. Jesus said we must ask God to forgive our sins. So, when we readily confess our sins, the blood of Jesus sanctifies us to have the boldness to approach God's throne for an effective prayer life (Heb. 10:1).

> *"If we confess our sins, he is faithful and just to forgive us our sins, and to cleanse us from all unrighteousness." — 1 John 1:9*

Similarly, we must forgive others who have wronged us (Matthew 7:12). Jesus said those who want God's forgiveness must forgive others. God will not forgive you if you do not forgive others (Matthew 18: 21-35). Therefore, we must repent from our hearts, confess our sins, and forgive those who have offended us.

> *"25And when ye stand praying, forgive, if ye have ought against any: that your Father also which is in heaven may forgive you your trespasses. 26But if ye do not forgive, neither will your Father which is in heaven forgive your trespasses." — Mark 11:25-26*

Thus, confessing our sins and forgiving others are significant for effective prayer. We should not gloss over sin (Gal. 5:13). Jesus had no sin, so He never asked for forgiveness. However, He forgave all wrongly accused and mistreated Him. Even on the cross, He asked God to forgive those who crucified Him. Likewise, intercessors must forgive others from our hearts so that God will forgive us our sins. Sin renders our prayers ineffective.

Petition

Just as we need "daily bread" for our physical wellbeing, we need daily deliverance from the evil and temptation we face daily. We need daily bread for sustenance. God is our provider, and He supplies all our needs. The model of prayer continues with a request for deliverance from evil and temptation. It is imperative to trust God to provide for our spiritual and temporal needs (Rom. 1:10; 2 Cor. 12:8). Jesus teaches us to pray for deliverance from evil and temptation since we cannot defeat the devil alone. We must acknowledge our limitations and call on God to step in and help us. The devil lurks everywhere, roaring and seeking to devour people.

> *"⁷Casting all your care upon him; for he careth for you. ⁸Be sober, be vigilant; because your adversary the devil, as a roaring lion, walketh about, seeking whom he may devour: ⁹Whom resist stedfast in the faith, knowing that the same afflictions are accomplished in your brethren that are in the world." — 1 Peter 5:7-9*

Thus, intercessors pray for God to deliver people from evil and temptation. We daily face the wickedness, snares, and the wiles of the devil, such as sin and its consequences, wars, diseases, lust, poverty, and all kinds of pain. Intercessors must stand in the gap for the deliverance of others, for our victory is in Jesus Christ. Jesus overcame the temptations of Satan with the word of God. He paid for all our sins and set us free, but the devil continues to buffet us with evil and his ungodly lures. However, God has empowered believers with His Word and the Holy Spirit to resist the devil and pray for others. For instance, the apostles interceded for the sick, demon-possessed, and people suffering from many afflictions of the devil.

*"¹²Therefore rejoice, ye heavens, and ye that dwell in them. Woe to the inhabiters of the earth and of the sea! for the devil is come down unto you, having great wrath, because he knoweth that he hath but a short time, ... ¹⁷And the dragon was wroth with the woman, and went to make war with the remnant of her seed, which keep the commandments of God, and have the testimony of Jesus Christ." — **Revelation 12:12, 17***

Additionally, intercessors must pray for the deliverance of lost souls and believers going through challenges in their Christian walk. The devil desires us to fail just as he fell from grace. So, he bedevils us with all kinds of evil and temptation in every aspect of life. He intended to derail Jesus' mission on earth with his temptations in the wilderness, but he failed. The devil also tempted Peter to deny Jesus after His arrest. But because Jesus prayed for Peter beforehand, he repented and fulfilled his given mandate to lead the early church.

*"³¹And the Lord said, Simon, Simon, behold, Satan hath desired to have you, that he may sift you as wheat: ³²But I have prayed for thee, that thy faith fails not: and when thou art converted, strengthen thy brethren." — **Luke 22:31-32***

However, intercessors must acknowledge that God will always answer prayers according to His will and time, and not what we desire. Therefore, we should submit our prayers and patiently wait and accept God's will. For example, Paul prayed three times for deliverance from a "thorn in the flesh," but God said His grace was enough for Paul to bear it (2 Corinthians 12:7-9).

Thanksgiving

To show oneself grateful, benefits or favors, especially to God. Jesus Christ always thanked God for answering His prayers before the results were physically manifested. He believed in the Father's love to answer His prayers. For example, Jesus thanked God for hearing Him before He prayed for Lazarus to rise from death.

> *"⁴¹Then they took away the stone from the place where the dead was laid. And Jesus lifted up his eyes, and said, Father, I thank thee that thou hast heard me. ⁴²And I knew that thou hearest me always: but because of the people which stand by I said it, that they may believe that thou hast sent me. ⁴³And when he thus had spoken, he cried with a loud voice, Lazarus, come forth. ⁴⁴And he that was dead came forth, bound hand and foot with graveclothes: and his face was bound about with a napkin. Jesus saith unto them, Loose him, and let him go."*
> *— John 11:41-44*

Similarly, Paul urged the Philippians to submit their prayers to God with thanksgiving. When we pray with thanksgiving instead of lamenting, we express faith in God to answer our prayers. Thus, intercessors must come before God with thanksgiving, acknowledging God's love and faithfulness in answering our prayer, no matter how dire the situation is.

> *"⁶Be careful for nothing; but in everything by prayer and supplication with thanksgiving let your requests be made known unto God. ⁷ᴬⁿᵈ the peace of God, which passeth all understanding, shall keep your hearts and minds through Christ Jesus."* *— Philippians 4:6-7*

Fasting

Fasting, in the Bible, means to voluntarily lessen or disregard the intake of food for a specific time and to seek divine guidance.

Before Jesus started His public ministry, He fasted for forty days in the wilderness. Being full of the Holy Ghost, He returned from Jordan (Matthew 4:2).

- He was led by the Spirit into the wilderness.
- Tempted by the devil for forty days.
- He ate nothing and hungered after the fast.

He also taught fasting must be in secret without a public show of sad countenance. When the Pharisees questioned why His disciples were not fasting, Jesus explained they would fast when He departed this earth.

> *"16Moreover when ye fast, be not, as the hypocrites, of a sad countenance: for they disfigure their faces, that they may appear unto men to fast. Verily I say unto you, They have their reward. 17But thou, when thou fastest, anoint thine head, and wash thy face; 18That thou appear not unto men to fast, but unto thy Father which is in secret: and thy Father, which seeth in secret, shall reward thee openly." — **Matthew 6:16-18**

After some of His disciples asked Him why they could not deliver the boy tormented by the deaf and dumb spirit (Mark 9 17-29). Jesus told them some situations could only be remedied by prayer and fasting.

> *"And he said unto them, This kind can come forth by nothing, but by prayer and fasting." — **Mark 9:29**

This means some situations call for both prayer and fasting. Therefore, fasting is an essential part of intercession. For instance, Cornelius was fasting and praying when he had a divine visitation that brought deliverance to him and his household (Acts 10:1-48). Also, the disciples of the early church always fasted and prayed before making significant decisions, such as selecting elders of the church. For example, as the church at Antioch fasted and prayed, God chose Barnabas and Paul for His work (Acts 13).

The body of Christ can accomplish much with prayer and fasting. When church leaders sought God's direction for their ministry through prayer and fasting, the Holy Spirit responded, "Set apart for me Barnabas and Saul for the work to which I have called them" (Acts 13:13). The churches in Galatia, when appointing elders to watch over the flock, fasted and prayed. We fast when dealing with temptations, beginning with God's work, and selecting and appointing elders and leaders.

Fasting humbles the soul, and the prayers of a humble person are more likely to be answered.

Jesus warned against fasting to show off. Prayer and fasting amount to nothing without obedience.

We humble ourselves before God in prayer. Fasting is essential today because Jesus said His disciples would fast when He was gone, and prayer with fasting effectively attracts God's blessing (Matthew 6:18).

Persistent Prayers

Persistent prayer means you pray until you get the answer from God. Jesus taught His disciples persistent prayers with the parable of a man who honored his friend's request for bread at midnight to feed his quests because of his persistence. He said the man gave bread to his friend not because of friendship but because of his persistence.

Thus, Jesus said when we ask, seek, and knock, our heavenly Father will answer our prayers. He explains that if sinful humans can give good things to their children, our heavenly Father is more willing to bless us. Blind Bartimaeus received his sight when he persistently called on Jesus to help him, even as the people shouted at him to keep quiet. Therefore, praying with persistence and expectation will yield the best results. Our faith in God's goodness makes us confident in asking for His gifts. A similar parable was about the widow who continuously asked the unjust judge to avenge her. Therefore, God wants us to pray with perseverance. Similarly, Jesus persisted in prayer three times in the garden of Gethsemane concerning the cross, and God answered according to His will (Matthew 26:36-46, Ephesians 6:18)

Persistent prayer shows determination to get results. For example, Paul prayed three times for God to deliver him, instead God assured him His grace was enough for him to endure.

God delights in answering our prayers when we persevere. We must submit to God's will and obey him as we persist. God's ways are right, not ours. However, our hearts may not understand His will or timing because our ways may differ from His. We must wait for God's answer to manifest. In faith and trusting God's goodness, we can consistently persevere in prayer.

Midnight prayers

Jesus did not provide a particular time for prayers. He commanded His disciples to watch and pray always to escape temptations. "Watch ye therefore, and pray always, that ye may be accounted worthy to escape all these things that shall come to pass, and to stand before the Son of Man" (Luke 21:36).

Prayer time is not limited to any specific period during the day or night. However, Jesus often prayed early at dawn to deepen His communion with God in private (Mark 1:35-38). For instance, Jesus prayed all night before He chose His disciples.

> "*12And it came to pass in those days, that he went out into a mountain to pray, and continued all night in prayer to God. 13And when it was day, he called unto him his disciples: and of them he chose twelve, whom also he named apostles;"* — *Luke 6:12-13*

Some of Jesus' teachings also revealed the spiritual significance of midnight. For instance, in the parable of the ten virgins, the bridegroom arrived at midnight (Matthew 25:6). Similarly, Paul and Silas received divine visitation and deliverance when they prayed and praised God in prison at midnight (Acts 16:25-34). Other midnight intercession and deliverance in the Bible include the following incidents:

- The parable of a man who honored his friend's request for bread at midnight to feed his quests because of his persistence (Luke 11:5).
- The bridegroom of the ten virgins came out at midnight (Matthew 25:6).

118

- Paul and Silas prayed and sang hymns of praise to God at midnight in prison and attracted God's presence that brought a great deliverance to the inmates, including the jailor (Acts 16:25-34).

- Paul and the people who were shipwrecked on the Adriatic Sea on their way to Rome had a mighty deliverance at midnight on the fourteenth day (Acts 27:27).

In Conclusion

God has given principles for effective intercession. He provided Moses with the model for priests in the Old Testament. The priests had the mandate to minister before God with sacrifices and offerings. The high priest stood in the gap and atoned for the sins of uncleanness in the Temple. However, the animal blood sacrifice could not cleanse the priests and Israel from unrighteousness.

Jesus, the eternal High Priest, washed our sins with His blood— something that the blood sacrifices of Levitical priests could not offer. He gave us the right to live in God's presence, offer spiritual sacrifices of praise, and enjoy an intimate fellowship with Him. Jesus satisfied all these requirements in the New Testament when He atoned for the sins of humanity and Himself with his blood. Jesus became the great High Priest and the ultimate intercessor. He imputed his righteousness to all believers and gave us a perfect model of prayer through Him to glorify God.

This chapter addressed the model of intercession, which encompasses praise, confession of sin, thanksgiving, and supplication, with the help of the Holy Spirit according to the will of God. The next chapter will discuss hindrances to effective intercession.

*If I **regard iniquity in my** heart, the Lord **will not hear** me —*

Psalm 66:18

5

Obstacles to Intercession

You are interceding for someone, but what renders your prayers ineffective? Is attack of the enemy a factor? God has stated in the Bible that disobedience to His Word is the only obstacle to our prayers. When Adam and Eve disobeyed His laws, He drove them out of the garden of Eden. Similarly, He rejected the sacrifices and offerings of some Levitical priests because of their disobedience.

> *"Behold, the LORD'S hand is not shortened, that it cannot save; neither his ear heavy, that it cannot hear: ² ᴮᵘᵗ your iniquities have separated between you and your God, and your sins have hid his face from you, that he will not hear."*
> *— Isaiah 59:2*

However, Jesus, the ultimate intercessor, satisfied all conditions to be the perfect High Priest. He obeyed all God's laws and communed daily with Him. So, God honored all His prayers. Jesus also cautioned that the disobedient cannot be fruitful and would be thrown out of God's Kingdom, but the prayers of the obedient will be answered (John 15:6-7).

> *"If a man abide not in me, he is cast forth as a branch, and is withered; and men gather them and cast them into the fire, and they are burned. If ye abide in me, and my words abide in you, ye shall ask what ye will, and it shall be done unto you."*
> *— John 15:6-7*

Obstacles to intercession in the Old Testament

The rebellion and fall of the first couple in the garden of Eden ruined their relationship and communion with God. Afterward, humanity faced hindrances in their communication with God. However, the merciful God always guided His people to return to Him in fellowship.

For instance, when God rejected Cain's unworthy offering, He urged him to offer a better one for acceptance (Genesis 4:7). Similarly, God instructed Moses on the requirements for acceptable and unacceptable sacrifices and offerings by the Levitical priests. He also commanded the priests not to appear before Him unholy, or else they die. Nevertheless, some priests disobeyed the Mosaic law and broke God's covenant with Israel. Thus, they could not perform their duty as intercessors creditably.

Hindrances According to the Law

Rebellion

Rebellion is a willful disobedience of God's word. God hates rebellion because it leads to the fall from grace. Those who disobey His laws face grave consequences. For instance, For instance, Lucifer was once an esteemed angel in heaven. But when he rebelled against God in heaven, was thrown down on earth, and became the devil. Similarly, the two sons of Aaron perished when they offered strange fire in the tabernacle, contrary to God's commandments.

God's hatred of rebellion manifested in the story of the pagan prophet Balaam. When the Moabite King Balak asked Him to curse the Israelites for fear of raiding him and his land, he proposed a gift to Balaam for his services. God warned him not to help or visit the Moabites, Israel's enemies, but he disobeyed until God ceded. Later, the Israelites slew him in battle (Numbers 22; Joshua 24).

Also, the prophet Samuel compared rebellion to witchcraft and idolatry when king Saul rebelled against the Lord (1 Samuel 15).

First, Saul was impatient and offered burned sacrifice and offering to the Lord because Samuel had delayed in coming to do the sacrifice. Saul was instructed to wait seven days for Samuel to arrive to give an offering to seek Lord's favor in battle. Instead, He went ahead of him and offered a sacrifice to God. He spared the life of king Agag and took the spoils of battle, though God commanded him to destroy the Amalekites and everything they possess.

Heaven will close its doors against us when we battle with God in rebellion. So, God rejected Saul and chose David as the king of Israel. Saul's disobedience enraged God's wrath, the Holy Spirit left him, and an evil spirit tormented him. Also, he consulted a witch to help him speak with the spirit of Samuel (1Samuel 13-16). Sadly, Saul died for his unfaithfulness against the Lord and because he consulted a medium for guidance. Besides, rebellion also shattered the life and destiny of King Saul. It is vital to obey God from the heart rather than to sacrifice.

You do not have to be stubborn when you have had the face of God turned away from you as He did from Saul. It is dangerous to disobey God. He refuses to answer your prayers or bless you. Trust God's goodwill always and surrender every situation to Him. There is never any need to be discouraged when the Holy Spirit is manifesting Himself to you and you know your prayers are heard. Moreover, answered prayer and obedience to the Father are intimately tied together.

Idolatry

Idolatry involves worshiping idols, images, a person, or anything other than the true God. It is the ultimate betrayal of God's relation with man and a severe offense against God. The first of the Ten Commandments,

> *"I am the Lord thy God, thou shalt not have any gods before Me,"* — ***Exodus 20.***

Explicitly prohibits idolatry. *All forms* of idolatry are unacceptable to God. It is contrary to "And thou shalt love the Lord thy God with all thine heart, and with all thy soul, and with all thy might" (Deut. 6:5).

For instance, God commanded Jacob and his household to get rid of their foreign gods before he arrived in Bethel and build an altar for Him. God wanted to destroy the Israelites as a nation when they worshipped the golden calf Aaron made, but Moses got rid of the molded image and interceded for Israel.

Israel had a covenant with God to serve Him alone. God told them to destroy the idols in Canaan. Yet, when the Israelites got to Canaan, they failed to destroy the idol temples there. Thus, they frequently turned to Canaanite religious practices that altered their worship of God, leading to idolatry. These pagan practices included sexual immorality, human sacrifices, and sacrificing unclean animals in the temple as part of their religious rituals. They failed to heed His repeated warnings and gave God's glory to idols. As a result, God allowed their enemies to overcome them. However, God always responded to Israel's cry for help and sent a judge or prophet to rescue them. Moses declared these false gods as demons. Demons are the powers behind idolatry; some of these practices include divination and

124

communicating with ungodly spiritual forces. For instance, Saul asked the witch at Endor to get Samuel back from the dead, and the witch saw a spirit rising from the ground, representing Samuel. God required His people to seek Him alone. Unfortunately, Israel copied these evil practices of the neighboring nations rather than their devotion to God's command.

Eventually, God divided Israel into two kingdoms, Judah, and Israel, after King Solomon worshipped idols. Solomon loved many foreign women who influenced him to build temples for their pagan gods.

God gave the northern kingdom, Israel, to Jeroboam, but he also led Israel to worship idols and forbade them from going to Jerusalem to worship. Jeroboam also built two golden calves and made priests of people who were not Levites. Also, king Ahab and his wife Jezebel were notable idol worshippers in Israel. These practices continued until the Assyrians destroyed Samaria and scattered the ten tribes. In the Northern kingdom, idolatry lasted nearly two centuries. Finally, the Assyrians conquered Israel and scattered the ten tribes according to God's decree. Nevertheless, many God-honoring kings lived in the southern kingdom of Judah, such as Hezekiah and Josiah. However, idolatry became common because of wicked kings like Manasseh. For instance, during the reign of King Zedekiah, some priests burned incense in high places, built altars for idols, and took part in defiling the temple. As a result, God sent prophets to warn His people that Jerusalem would also be destroyed. Despite these warnings, idolatry continued until God finally fulfilled His prophecy through King Nebuchadnezzar of Babylon, who captured them and destroyed the temple.

Filthy Garments

God required the priests to wear holy garments before they ministered before Him. As a sign of their worthiness, they had to bathe and wear holy clothes as prescribed by God, or else they would die. God gave a detailed description of the priests' spotless garments (Exodus 28). These were sacred garments for Aaron and his sons for service.

> *"The woven garments as well, and the holy garments for Aaron the priest, and the garments of his sons, with which to carry on their priesthood." — Exodus 31:10*

So, the priests had to wash from any uncleanness before wearing the holy garments. They could touch nothing unclean. For instance, when the two sons of Aaron died, God commanded him not to defile himself with their dead bodies (Leviticus 10:1-7). Also, Satan resisted Joshua, the high priest, because he had filthy clothes. Sin defiled his garment and made him unworthy before God. He needed holy clothes without spots or wrinkles to approach God. So Satan tormented him, and he was ineffective as an intercessor for Israel. But God had mercy on him. He rebuked Satan and gave Joshua a new garment (Zechariah 3:1-8). God also commanded the priests not to defile themselves with alcoholic beverages.

> *"⁸ And the LORD spake unto Aaron, saying, ⁹Do not drink wine nor strong drink, thou, nor thy sons with thee, when ye go into the tabernacle of the congregation, lest ye die: it shall be a statute for ever throughout your generations: ¹⁰And that ye may put difference between holy and unholy, and between unclean and clean;" — Leviticus 10:8-10*

Ungodly family life

God instituted marriage as a lifetime union when He created the world. Marriage is a covenanted union between a man and a woman. He created marriage to provide man with a helpmate for companionship and procreation to expand His kingdom on earth. God commands His children to be faithful to the marriage covenant and so forbade Israel to marry Gentiles because they would lure them to serve their idols.

> *"Neither shalt thou make marriages with them; thy daughter thou shalt not give unto his son, nor his daughter shalt thou take unto thy son. ⁴For they will turn away thy son from following me, that they may serve other gods: so will the anger of the LORD be kindled against you, and destroy thee suddenly." — Deut. 7:3-4*

However, the priests of Judah maltreated their wives and married strange women during the time of Malachi. They were fraudulent, deceitful, offensive, abusive, and their covenant design for marriage by violence. Therefore, God rejected their prayers and sacrifice (Malachi 2:1-16).

> *"¹² The LORD will cut off the man that doeth this, the master and the scholar, out of the tabernacles of Jacob, and him that offereth an offering unto the LORD of hosts.. ¹³And this have ye done again, covering the altar of the LORD with tears, with weeping, and with crying out, insomuch that he regardeth not the offering any more, or receiveth it with good will at your hand. ¹⁴Yet ye say, Wherefore? Because the LORD hath been witness between thee and the wife of thy youth, against whom thou hast dealt treacherously: yet is she thy companion, and the wife of thy covenant." — Malachi 2:11-14*

In the same way, after Judah returned to Jerusalem from Babylon, some priests and Levites defiled themselves by marrying Gentiles. However, Ezra stood in the gap and led the people to repent of their evil ways. Therefore, those who married gentiles sent them away (Ezra 9:1-2). Second, God commanded the Israelites to teach their children His laws, so they walk in His ways. God praised Abraham that he would guide his children and household in the ways of the Lord (Genesis 18:19). Not only did Abraham keep the commandments, but he taught his household to do so, too. God also said priests whose daughters live ungodly lives defile their fathers (Leviticus 21:9).

> *"⁶And these words, which I command thee this day, shall be in thine heart: ⁷And thou shalt teach them diligently unto thy children, and shalt talk of them when thou sittest in thine house, and when thou walkest by the way, and when thou liest down, and when thou risest up." — **Deuteronomy 6:6-7.***

However, the children of some priests led an ungodly life. For instance, Eli was the high priest of Shiloh, but his sons perverted the laws of God and rebelled against Him. They took the offerings and sacrifices meant for God for their gain and committed sexual immorality with women in the Temple, but Eli failed to keep them in check. Thus, Eli died with his two sons, and God took away the priesthood from his house. God chastised Eli and his two sons for profaning the Temples' holy vessels (1 Sam 2:22-36). Similarly, Samuel appointed his sons Abijah and Joel as judges over Israel as he grew old. However, they did not walk in his ways but perverted justice and took bribes. Samuel was a successful intercessor for Israel, but his disobedient children did not take after him. So the people requested for a king to rule over them (1 Samuel 8:1-22).

Contaminated Vessels

God's Temple had a variety of vessels made of gold, silver, brass, and copper. These holy vessels contained oil, ashes, spices, precious ointments, bread, and other items which the priests used in performing daily and seasonal ministerial services.

Therefore, these vessels were holy to the Lord, and He allowed only the priests and Levites to handle these holy items. However, some kings of Judah despised the holy vessels, contrary to the laws. They showed no difference between the sacred and unholy. Thus, they desecrated the holy receptacles, and God punished them. For instance, King Ahaz of Judah desecrated the vessels, and God delivered him to the hands of his enemies.

> *"24And Ahaz gathered together the vessels of the house of God, and cut in pieces the vessels of the house of God, and shut up the doors of the house of the LORD, and he made him altars in every corner of Jerusalem. 25And in every several city of Judah he made high places to burn incense unto other gods, and provoked to anger the LORD God of his fathers." — 2* ***Chronicles 28:24, 25***

Subsequently, the temple's vessels ended up in Babylon following Nebuchadnezzar's invasion of Jerusalem and destruction of the temple (Daniel 1:1-2). However, God punished King Belshazzar of Babylon for using the holy vessels as drinking cups for his party.

The King and his entourage praised the gods of gold and silver, brass, iron, wood, and stone as they used these holy vessels. Consequently, the King was overthrown by King Darius that night. Later, King Cyrus, Darius' successor, gave the vessels to Zerubbabel to be sent back to Jerusalem.

Unworthy Sacrifice

God demanded perfect sacrifices and offerings. Thus, He had specific laws and requirements for acceptable animals for sacrifice and fresh products for offerings. The priests offered animal sacrifices to atone for the sins of the people. They were to bring unblemished animals for sacrifice, but some dishonored God and brought sick animals and polluted bread (Malachi 1:6-8).

> *"You shall not sacrifice to the Lord your God an ox or a sheep which has a blemish or any defect, for that is a detestable thing to the Lord your God." — **Deuteronomy 17:1***

Therefore, God detested their sacrifices. He compared what they offered to Him and what they gave to their leaders. He condemned the Israelites for their lack of respect.

> *"'When you offer blind animals in sacrifice, is that not evil? And when you offer those that are lame or sick, is that not evil? Present that to your governor; will he accept you or show you favor?' says the LORD of hosts." — **Malachi 1:8***

God is worthy of our best in our offerings and sacrifices. Malachi warned against treating the sacrifices and offerings with disregard. He also cautioned that God rejects such sacrifices without a blessing. It is important to worship, but it is essential to do it according to His laws.

Maltreatment of the less privileged

God commanded the priests to be fair without discrimination against the poor, especially in passing judgment. He also told them to care for the poor, strangers, orphans, and widows (Leviticus 25:47-48; Deuteronomy 10:18).

- "Do not pervert justice; do not show partiality to the poor or favoritism to the great but judge your neighbor fairly." Lev. 19:15

- "He defends the cause of the fatherless and the widow, and loves the alien, giving him food and clothing." Deuteronomy 10:18

- "Cursed *be* he that perverteth the judgment of the stranger, fatherless, and widow. And all the people shall say, Amen." — Deuteronomy 27:19

  "The heads thereof judge for reward, and the priests thereof teach for hire, and the prophets thereof divine for money: yet will they lean upon the LORD, and say, Is not the LORD among us? none evil can come upon us. ¹²*Therefore shall Zion for your sake be plowed as a field, and Jerusalem shall become heaps, and the mountain of the house as the high places of the forest." — Micah 3:11-12*

However, some priests practiced extortion, perpetuated robbery, mistreated the widows, persecuted the impoverished, oppressed strangers, denied justice, and lied about visions and divinations. God's commandments are against those who mistreat the less privileged in society. Prophet Micah warned of God's judgment against Jerusalem because the leaders and priests maltreated the people.

Ungodly Alliances and Help

God specifically told the Israelites not to make any covenant with the people in Canaan, but to drive them out utterly. God knew that if the inhabitants remained, their evil practices would destroy His people.

> *Then the Lord said: "I am making a covenant with you. Before all your people I will do wonders never before done in any nation in all the world. The people you live among will see how awesome is the work that I, the Lord, will do for you. Obey what I command you today. I will drive out before you the Amorites, Canaanites, Hittites, Perizzites, Hivites and Jebusites. Be careful not to make a treaty with those who live in the land where you are going, or they will be a snare among you." — **Exodus 34:10-12:***

Judah had only one covenant with God. Yet, they violated the covenant when they sought help and protection aside from God.

> *Then the men of Israel took some of their provisions; but they did not ask counsel of the Lord. So Joshua made peace with them, and made a covenant with them to let them live; and the rulers of the congregation swore to them. — **Joshua 9: 14-15***

God defended Israel when they called upon Him, but some kings made unholy alliances and sought help from Egypt, Damascus, and other neighboring nations—a violation of God's word that brought consequences. We must not seek ungodly help in difficult times because it leads to defeat. It is against God's terms and attracts His fury (Isaiah 31:1-9).

Defiling the Sabbath

God commanded the Israelites to keep the Sabbath holy. They had to work for six days and rest on the seventh day. Likewise, the land should have its rest in the seventh year without cultivation. He blessed them when they observe the Sabbath. Later, both Israel and Judah refused to observe the Sabbath day. Eventually, God sent Judah into captivity so the land could have its Sabbath.

*"But if ye will not hearken unto me to hallow the sabbath day, and not to bear a burden, even entering in at the gates of Jerusalem on the sabbath day; then will I kindle a fire in the gates thereof, and it shall devour the palaces of Jerusalem, and it shall not be quenched." — **Jeremiah 17:27***

*Yet the house of Israel rebelled against Me in the wilderness; they did not walk in My statutes; they despised My judgments, 'which, if a man does, he shall live by them; and they defiled My Sabbaths. Then I said I would pour out My fury on them in the wilderness, to consume them. — **Ezekiel 20:13***

*"[19]And they burnt the house of God, and brake down the wall of Jerusalem, and burnt all the palaces thereof with fire, and destroyed all the goodly vessels thereof. [20]And them that had escaped from the sword carried he away to Babylon; where they were servants to him and his sons until the reign of the kingdom of Persia: [21]To fulfill the word of the LORD by the mouth of Jeremiah, until the land had enjoyed her sabbaths: for as long as she lay desolate she kept sabbath, to fulfill threescore and ten years." — **2 Chronicles 36:19-21***

Extortion

God forbade extortion and excessive usury to prevent the exploitation of a poor Israelite since insolvency caused slavery in Israel. An extortioner is guilty of seizing from another by strife, greed, and oppression that does not lawfully belong to him. Prophet Micah warned Jerusalem would become desolate because the priests and judges practiced extortion.

> *"The heads thereof judge for reward, and the priests thereof teach for hire, and the prophets thereof divine for money: yet will they lean upon the LORD, and say, Is not the LORD among us? none evil can come upon us. ¹²Therefore shall Zion for your sake be plowed as a field, and Jerusalem shall become heaps, and the mountain of the house as the high places of the forest," —- Micah 3:11-12*

Also, Naboth had a vineyard close to King Ahab's palace in the city of Jezreel. Although Ahab desired to acquire the vineyard for his vegetable garden, Naboth refused to sell it to Ahab since he inherited the land from his ancestors. Enraged by this Naboth decision, Jezebel plotted with Naboth's city's folk. They accused Naboth of slandering God and dishonoring the king. Therefore, the people stoned him and told Jezebel he was dead. She sent a message to Ahab telling him the news. Ahab then went to Naboth's vineyard to take it (1 Kings 1-16).

Moreover, a warning against extortion, Elijah visited Ahab and prophesied his death and the extermination of the Ahab's descendants' bond or free. He also prophesied the death of Jezebel. However, Ahab humbled himself at Elijah's words, and God spared the king.

Obstacles to intercession in the New Testament

Jesus Christ, the ultimate intercessor, met all the divine requirements to be the eternal High Priest, unlike the Levitical priesthood. Jesus fully obeyed God's commandments and exhibited godly qualities like love, peace, compassion, patience, and obedience in His intercessory ministry. He forgave sinners; healed, delivered the oppressed, and accomplished His ultimate intercession on the cross in the face of opposition from His people. Jesus gave grace and treated others with respect and goodness. He let go of offenses, relying on God's love. While fully God and man, Jesus never sinned. He submitted to the will of God for the salvation of humanity. The heathen rulers found Him innocent during his trial, affirming His godliness. All true believers are now priests unto God, taking unto them the righteousness of Jesus with complete devotion in fear of the Lord. Jesus has made a way for all believers and taught us how to pray to the Father. Believers are God's Temple, equipped with the Holy Spirit to lead a disciplined and holy life, free from the power of sin. Jesus showed us the perfect way to worship God. He told the Samaritan women God seeks people to worship Him in spirit and truth, and not on mount Sinai or Jerusalem (John 4).

> *"⁷If ye abide in me, and my words abide in you, ye shall ask what ye will, and it shall be done unto you. ⁸Herein is my Father glorified, that ye bear much fruit; so shall ye be my disciples?"* — ***John 15:7-8***

Depraved attitudes negatively affect our services, and prayers become ineffective. However, when we acknowledge and confess our sins with repentant hearts, God sets us free. Jesus said that disobedience to His word would hinder our prayers.

Steps to Resolve Hindrances Jesus Warned Against:

1. Disobedience

Jesus said our prayers will be answered if we obey His word (John 15). Disobedience always deters our prayers, while obedience to God's word allows us to approach Him according to His will.

> *"6 If a man abide not in me, he is cast forth as a branch, and is withered; and men gather them, and cast them into the fire, and they are burned. If ye abide in me, and my words abide in you, ye shall ask what ye will, and it shall be done unto you."*
> — *John 15:6-7*

We honor God when we obey His commandments, and He honors us by answering our prayers. Disobedience dishonors God, and it affects our prayers. He frowns on acting contrary to these laws and punishes those who do so. Scriptures demands we accept the authority and will of God. Therefore, disobedience is a sin of rebellion, refusing to come under the authority of someone above and distrusting God. Our close relationship with God gives us personal instructions aligned with His Word. However, when we make decisions He disapproves of, we are disobeying Him and causing a split in our relationship with Him. We are hindered from praying if we willfully reject God's word and refuse to receive the Holy Spirit. Rebellion is considered witchcraft by God. The Holy Spirit is grieved by rebellion, so He becomes our enemy and starts fighting us. Disobedience will always hinder our prayers, whereas obedience to God's word enables us to approach Him with requests according to His will. Disobeying God prevents us from asking for answers against His Will. Sometimes, our prayers are unanswered, but God has better plans for us. He knows what is in our hearts and is best for a person's future life (1 John 3:21-24).

2. Flee Idolatry - You shall have no other gods before me

God hates and does not tolerate idolatry because He would not share His glory with anybody or anything. Worshipping or esteeming anything or anybody above God is idolatry. Jesus said no one can worship two masters in sincerity, citing God and money.

> *"Jesus said, No man can serve two masters: for either he will hate the one and love the other; or else he will hold to the one, and despise the other. Ye cannot serve God and mammon."* — **Matthew 6:24**

The New Testament warns that putting ourselves, our families, positions, possessions, or talents above God violates His commandments. Similarly, the love of money replaces the love of God. Jesus asked the rich young ruler to sell all his property and give the proceeds to the poor, and then be his disciple, but he went away in sorrow because he was very rich. He chose his riches over salvation. Jesus said it is difficult for those who trust in riches to enter the kingdom of God (Mark 10:17:27)

> *"He that loveth father or mother more than me is not worthy of me: and he that loveth son or daughter more than me is not worthy of me."* — **Matthew 10:37**

Anything we desire more than God results in idolatry, as they replace the love of God in our hearts. Ungodly church doctrines and hero worship of religious leaders lead to idolatry. Instead of the Holy Spirit leading us, our ungodly desires become our passion because God's love has been substituted in our hearts by something else. The genuine worship of God is exclusive. Thus, to avoid gods of wealth and the traditions of men, we must love God with all our hearts and place Him first in everything we do.

3. Lack of knowledge of God's word

God answers prayers according to His will, and only His word reveals His will. Therefore, if we do not know the Word, we will not know His will, and our prayers will be ineffective. Jesus' ministry was successful because He interceded according to His will based on God's commandment.

Thus, intercessors must be students of the word so we can pray according to His will. When Satan tempted Jesus, He used the word to overturn his evil plans. Note that Satan even quoted the word to confuse Jesus. So, if we do not know the word, the devil can deceive us, and we may pray contrary to His will. There have been and continue to be all kinds of waves and doctrines contrary to the word. The Holy Spirit helps us understand God's word by revealing divine truths to us.

> *"15Study to shew thyself approved unto God, a workman that needeth not to be ashamed, rightly dividing the word of truth."* — **2 Timothy 2:15**

> *"14That we henceforth be no more children, tossed to and fro, and carried about with every wind of doctrine, by the sleight of men, and cunning craftiness, whereby they lie in wait to deceive;"* — **Ephesians 4:14**

If we are ignorant of God's word, we will be deceived by doctrines. For instance, Paul persecuted the church, thinking he was serving God because he did not know about the salvation Jesus has brought to humanity. He followed the Pharisees and stuck to the law of Moses. We must meditate on His word to enable us to pray rightly. Hearing God correctly leads to obedience and effective prayers (John 5:19).

4. Unbelief

Faith in God's love to answer our prayers is key to effective prayers. God requires us to believe in His goodness through Jesus. Therefore, unbelief will render our prayers unanswered. The Nazarenes did not believe in Jesus, so they could not experience many miracles by Jesus (Mark 6:1-6). Jesus told His disciples they could not deliver the dumb boy because of their unbelief.

> *"[19]Then came the disciples to Jesus apart, and said, Why could not we cast him out? [20] And Jesus said unto them, Because of your unbelief: for verily I say unto you, If ye have faith as a grain of mustard seed, ye shall say unto this mountain, Remove hence to yonder place; and it shall remove; and nothing shall be impossible unto you." — **Matthew 17:19-20**

We can only increase our faith as we read and meditate on the word of God (Romans 10:17). Accepting God's word in Christ must be unconditional. Jesus was amazed at some people's unbelief as He taught them, including some Jewish leaders. He was also enthralled by what he heard from centurion seeking healing spoke to him, "Lord; I am not worthy that Thou shouldest come under my roof: but speak the word only, and my servant shall be healed" (Matthew 8:8-10). Jesus was, however, amazed at some people's unbelief as he taught in villages. He warned, some Jewish leaders will not enter the kingdom since they had resigned in unbelief. We must overcome unbelief through the daily reading of God's word. Prayer is powerless without faith. But Jesus said with faith, we can handle insurmountable situations. There is nothing you could not tackle. James also said if we waiver, we cannot receive anything from God.

Dishonoring God

In the Bible, reverence is considered an honor and inherent respect. Unfortunately, prayer is often hindered when we disrespect the Father whom we pray to, the Holy Spirit, or the Son whom we pray through. Inconsistencies in our lives can cause this disrespect. Unsurprisingly, God's children have difficulties praying if they fail to obey His will.

The desire to pray becomes obstructed. To unveil your heart, you must believe in your heavenly Father. When you lack love, faith, and reverence for God, are cold-hearted towards Him, and lack faith in that vast willing heart waiting to bless you, they can choke your prayers. Whenever a man is in communion with the Almighty Father, and the words "Abba, Father" become part of language, he will gain the favor of God when he asks with confidence in someone he trusts implicitly and whose Will he values. Prayer suffers the most if a man is not at peace with God.

Without Jesus, through whom we pray, if we are self-righteous; if we pursue our interests without considering the love of the Father; and if we follow the Pharisees in their complacency, our prayers will be hindered. Those who do not follow His example, share His loving spirit, and crucify Him again and expose Him to open shame will be hindered in their prayers. You cannot plead in court if you have quarreled with an Advocate. Your prayers are meaningless without the ultimate intercessor offering them on your behalf.

The same is true of the Holy Spirit. The Spirit writes the prayer in our hearts first before God accepts it. Prayer is not as much about us as God interceding for us through the Spirit. If we grieve the Spirit, we cannot pray. If we pray with the Spirit, we cannot pray against what

God's Word says. We do so because our supplications are against the Spirit's loving nature. The divine Comforter must be at the forefront of your mind. If He is not at the forefront of your mind, He will sound speechless to you. He will not help you pray if you do not yield to Him in other areas of your life.

> *"Then the Lord said, 'Because this people draw near with their words and honor Me with their lip service, But they remove their hearts far from Me, And their reverence for Me consists of tradition learned by man.'"* — **Isaiah 29:11**

So, we cannot trifle with the approach to the Mercy Seat or make a point of serving sin. "You ask and receive not because you ask amiss, that you may consume it upon your lusts." Without our cooperation, He cannot walk in harmony with us. In trouble, scripture implores Christians to take the right path and do what is right. We must endure that bravely and then pray to God, "Lord, by Your grace, I have chosen that straight and honest path, help me now," and He will. As Christians, I pray that God grants us grace to walk with Him in power. We are to rest only on Jesus, and may He empower us to pray.

God's children, who know how to pray mightily, can be one with God's heart and are God's hands at work among them. God is present in them. The Lord, however, is jealous of those who love Him most; thus, he must observe caution and keep watch. Living humbly and approaching God with humility will not cause obstacles to your prayers.

8. Unconfessed Sin

God is holy, and He cannot behold sin. Unconfessed sin grieves the Holy Spirit and hinders our prayers. The merciful God knows we are fallible, and that is why He has made provisions for us to repent when we sin. Jesus paid for our sins, and so God will forgive us when we confess our sins to Him. Therefore, we must be quick to repent and ask for forgiveness when we falter. Only true repentance can restore our fellowship with God. When we confess our sins in prayer to our Heavenly Father, He forgives and cleanses us to avoid hindrance to our communion with Him. Jesus told the church in Ephesus to repent of their shortcomings, or else He would remove their candlestick (Revelation 2:5).

> *"14For if ye forgive men their trespasses, your heavenly Father will also forgive you: But if ye forgive not men their trespasses, neither will your Father forgive your trespasses."*
> — *Matthew 6:14-15*

Also, Jesus said if we do not forgive others their sins, God will not forgive us. Our prayer is fruitless unless we forgive others. Jesus forgave all those who wronged Him. We must choose to forgive others and not hold resentment in our hearts, just as God has forgiven us. Do not let Satan keep you in the bondage of bitterness and resentment. Forgive others regardless of their response to you.

Your godly example makes others aware of God's grace and mercy. Forgiving others sets you free from hurt and shuts doors to the enemy in your life. Our prayer is fruitless unless we forgive others. We open spiritual doors and allow demons to harass us. Spiritual defilement brings destruction. It also attracts God's punishment and desolation.

Unforgiveness

Unforgiveness grieves God and hinders the answer to prayers. When someone hurts or betrays you, breaks your trust, or causes intense emotional pain, you cannot release that person. It is a sin that causes bitterness and destroys our lives. When we confess our sins in prayer to our Heavenly Father, He forgives and cleanses us to avoid hindrance to our communion with Him. Our prayer is fruitless unless we forgive others.

The need for salvation is a glorious transaction of all our sins laid on Jesus. It is deception after salvation and not the truth to say we do not have sin (1 John 1:8). Jesus still hates the sin in us. If our sin is neither pardoned nor cleansed out daily, our supplication is blocked since we must be holy to approach God. Grieving the Holy Spirit taints our testimony. Jesus warned against unforgiveness so that we can be cleaned daily with the renewal of communion and fullness of the Holy Spirit. Thus, we cannot live without the confession of sin.

We live in a world of filth, so daily confession of uncleanness is necessary to wholeness as children of God. Yet unforgiveness prevents our prayers from being answered. A terrible sin is refusing to forgive others, holding grudges, or harboring hatred toward others (Matthew 6:14-15; 18:21-35). Additionally, forgiveness without faith leads to losing communion with God and broken relationships with people. We must humble ourselves to forgive another (1 Peter 3:7). The act of not treating one's wife with love and care will hinder the intercessory prayer. The same applies to wives who do not honor their husbands. The only way to overcome our sins is to confess them to God. God does not take delight in those who stubbornly hold on to offenses. Obstacles to prayer can emanate from broken relations among parents, husbands, wives, and children in the family (Eph. 4:3).

Furthermore, Jesus warns Peter, the other disciples, and believers about failure to forgive others (Matthew 18). He added God will deliver His children into the hands of tormentors. He will let them suffer in misery with obstructed prayers and subject them to the torments of the soul. Embittered believers made shipwrecks of their lives, endangered by facing terrible consequences. Forgiveness must come from our hearts like Jesus forgave and prayed for people who crucified and mocked Him while He died, yet He prayed, "Father, forgive them; for they know not what they do." The Bible warns, "But if ye do not forgive, neither will your Father which is in heaven forgive your trespasses" (Mark 11:25-26). We are to forgive and make peace as Jesus did with a pure heart.

Unforgiveness in the heart is the wall of sins before God, and prayer cannot get through until we forgive others. So, search your heart daily before sundown to judge every grudge of unforgiveness and confess to God and repent. God will take it out and cleanse it to be forgiven. Release others from the debt owed to remove the wedge between the other person and God and us. Finally, unforgiveness is a rebellion of not setting other people free, tormenting, and destructive, which can turn into strongholds and targets for the enemy to destroy our lives. So, the challenge is to search and examine our lives of bitterness, forgive, pray, and ask God to reveal any past hurts and rejection from others and ask Him to lose you from it.

Intercessors must choose to forgive others, just as God has forgiven them, and confront offenses with forgiveness instead of holding resentment in the heart. Offer forgiveness to the offenders and leave the rest to God, since past hurts will never escape the sight of the Lord. Do not let Satan keep you in the bondage of unforgiveness. Instead, forgive others regardless of their response to you.

Ungodly family life

God formed man and woman and gave them a family to bless the world. He also blesses them with their progeny. He commands husbands the men to love and honor their wives, as Christ loved the church and died for it. As precious weaker vessel and delicate gifts. Men must know their wives deeply and live with them, understanding their wives. A husband should be an example to his wife and bring up their children in a godly way.

He also commands wives to submit to their husbands as the church to Christ. Jesus warned divorce was never a part of God's plan for marriage. Mary was full of faith, humility, and devotion. Ruth had an attitude of humility. Elizabeth was full of the Holy Spirit. Priscilla was hospitable and passionate about helping others. Children are also commanded to obey their parents in the Lord, with a promise of prosperity and long life on the earth

However, ungodly family life violates Christ's instructions for domestic life and hinders prayers. Disharmony in the household, grieves God. Thus, couples must also submit to each other in honor, as husbands lead their wives.

When the husband neglects his duties towards the weaker partner and lacks support, compassion, and understanding for his wife, he violates God's laws. Such a slackened husband, priest, and intercessor of the home will find his prayers unanswered. Likewise, the wife's lack of honor can hinder prayers. Husbands and the head of the family avoid compromising your leadership with inadequate rationalizations. Husbands and wives must quickly reconcile, since God does not like strife. So, we must advise children who rebel against their parents, since the rebellion turns away the face of God (Matthew 5:23).

> *"Likewise, ye husbands, dwell with them according to knowledge, giving honor unto the wife, as unto the weaker vessel, and as being heirs together of the grace of life; that your prayers be not hindered." — 1 Peter 3:7*

However, the helpmate may seem like the one who bears it. But if there is a crisis, it is the man who must help, or else your blessings are being stolen. Men must fulfill their responsibility as heads of their houses. They are at their most effective when pushed to the limit. Yet, they maintain a permanent and loving presence in their lives by supporting their wife and providing appropriate monitoring and discipline for their children (Proverbs 31:10-12). Men should practice righteous conduct in front of others. If you let God be your delight, He will give you what you want (Psalm 37:4). You must also not pretend to be something you are not. We must act based on what we believe. Intercessors must be good stewards of the spiritual, emotional, and physical well-being of their family, including children God has entrusted to their care. The children of the priests must not engage in any uncleanness.

Unless you lead your family daily in the word, you will not produce good fruits but thorns. If someone hears the Word but does not act on it, he is like a man who looks in a mirror at himself. For once he has done that and gone, he immediately forgets who he is. Yet, when we follow the perfect law, the law of liberty, we will be blessed, not forgetting what we have heard, but acting upon the law. We must act based on what we believe. The family members with intercessory duties must be good stewards of the spiritual, emotional, and physical well-being of their family, including the children God has entrusted to their care. The children of the priests must not engage in any uncleanness.

Offenses

Offenses come when we face persecution and trials because of the word of God, leading to unfruitfulness (Mark 4:17). For example, John the Baptist was offended, and questioned Jesus after Herod imprisoned him. Jesus warned afflictions would come, but we should not be offended. Jesus was never annoyed or resentful because of a perceived insult, violation, or disregard for one's standards or principles.

Those around him could not offend Him, but He focused on what God thought about him. He overlooked faults in having compassion for people. He suffered as He preached the gospel. He overlooked faults and focused on His mission on earth. Jesus did not do many miracles in Galilee because the people were offended and questioned where Jesus got His authority from as they knew His parents (Matthew 13:54-58). When the Romans arrested Jesus, many disciples became offended and fled from Him. In the parable of the sower, Jesus taught that offense because of persecution will make us unfruitful in the kingdom of God. Intercessors must cultivate and maintain an unruffled heart to overcome offenses.

> *"Yet hath he not root in himself, but dureth for a while: for when tribulation or persecution ariseth because of the word, by and by he is offended." — **Matthew 13:21***

Unfortunately, the offense has gained ascendancy, sweeping through society. As conscious, mature adults, our hearts must not be easily offended. Our love for ourselves should not be more important than our love for others. Intercessors must cultivate and maintain an unruffled heart to avoid many of the enemy's deceptions. To accomplish our divine mission, we must come to the unity of faith with humility and reconciliation. Love is not touchy or provoked easily by anger. So, we don't have to be quick to argue and defend ourselves, quick to get angry, get hurt easily, and get resentful. In addition, it is glorious to overlook an offense (Pro. 19:11; 1 Cor. 13:5-6).

> *"³ Take heed to yourselves: If thy brother trespass against thee, rebuke him; and if he repents, forgive him. ⁴ And if he trespasses against thee seven times in a day, and seven times in a day turn again to thee, saying, I repent; thou shalt forgive him."* — **Luke 17:3-4**

Extortion

Jesus never acted nor obtained another's money or property through deception, force, fraud, forgery, intimidation, threat, or oppression. He did not take advantage of the poor, the ignorant, the innocent, the unsuspecting, and sometimes even family and friends to get more and more. Jesus condemns us as guilty of exploiting one another and forbids all types of stealing and fraud. Extortion was prevalent in His day, like Zacchaeus. Jesus warned and said,

> *"Woe unto you, scribes and Pharisees, hypocrites! for ye make clean the outside of the cup and of the platter, but within they are full of extortion and excess."* — **Matthew 23:25**

Simon of Samaria offered money to Peter for the empowerment of the Holy Spirit, but Peter warned him that the gift of the Holy Spirit was not for sale. Peter further urged Simon to repent of this evil intention so God would forgive him (Acts 8:5-24). Therefore, intercessors must not merchandise the gifts God has freely given us for the service of humanity. Willingly, we must serve, and God will supply all our needs.

Impatience

God answers prayers according to His will and timing. We cannot coerce God to satisfy our desires. Therefore, we must follow God's guidance and patiently wait for Him to answer our prayers. Impatience will cause us to murmur or seek unanswered questions. quick solutions. We must pray and leave the rest in God's hands, believing He will answer us in His perfect time. The devil offered Jesus a shortcut to fulfill His mandate on earth, but He rejected it and patiently endured the cross to accomplish God's will for humanity. Likewise, the devil will offer you a shortcut if you are impatient.

> *"8Again, the devil taketh him up into an exceeding high mountain, and sheweth him all the kingdoms of the world, and the glory of them; 9And saith unto him, All these things will I give thee, if thou wilt fall down and worship me. 10Then saith Jesus unto him, Get thee hence, Satan: for it is written, Thou shalt worship the Lord thy God, and him only shalt thou serve. 11 Then the devil leaveth him, and, behold, angels came and ministered unto him."* — ***Matthew 4:8-11***

Jesus also illustrated the importance of patience and persistence in the parable below:

"1And he spake a parable unto them to this end, that men ought always to pray, and not to faint; 2Saying, 'There was in a city a judge, which feared not God, neither regarded man: 3And there was a widow in that city; and she came unto him, saying, Avenge me of mine adversary. 4And he would not for a while: but afterward, he said within himself, Though I fear not God, nor regard man; 5Yet because this widow troubled me, I will avenge her, lest by her continual coming she weary

149

me'. [6] And the Lord said, 'Hear what the unjust judge saith. [7] And shall not God avenge his own elect, which cry day and night unto him, though he bear long with them? [8] I tell you that he will avenge them speedily. Nevertheless, when the Son of man cometh, shall he find faith on the earth?'" — **Luke 18:1-8**

In Conclusion:

Intercessors must avoid anything that impedes their prayers, such as idolatry, disobedience, unbelief, extortion, ungodly family life, impatience, offenses, and unconfessed sin. Some of the Old Testament priests showed no reverence to God by offering imperfect sacrifices and maltreating their wives, and the less privileged in their midst, so they were not effective intercessors.

However, in the New Testament, Jesus, the ultimate intercessor obeyed God and received answers to His prayers. Jesus warned His disciples about the condemnable sins such as unbelief, offense, and many others that render prayers unanswered. Therefore, these identified hindrances must be confessed and eliminated.

In the next chapter, we learn that Jesus led the ultimate revival of humanity when He paid for our sins and reconciled our hearts with God. He gave us His righteousness for our devoted service to God and mandated believers to continue the ministry of intercession and reconciliation to save the lost souls.

Wilt thou not revive us again: that thy people may rejoice in thee? 7 Shew us thy mercy, O LORD, and grant us thy salvation. 8 I will hear what God the LORD will speak: for he will speak peace unto his people, and to his saints: but let them not turn again to folly. — **Psalms 85:6-13**

6

Revive Us Again

The main reason for intercession is revival. The ultimate revival was the supernatural restoration of God-man fellowship with the outpouring of God's spirit on man.

The fall in the garden of Eden brought spiritual death. Thus, God initiated intercession to restore the lost souls of the sinful humanity. He gives the conditions and the specific scriptures to regenerate the soul. Self-effort cannot help; every step must depend on Him. God usually uses anointed chosen vessels to lead the people to repentance and revival. For example, under the Old Covenant, He used prophets and priests to preach repentance for revival in Israel. However, these revivals were short-lived because the people returned to their wickedness after enjoying freedom. They usually did this after the intercessor died.

> *"For God so loved the world, that he gave his only begotten Son, that whosoever believeth in him should not perish, but have everlasting life." — **John 3:16***

At the time appointed, Jesus led the ultimate revival for humanity when He paid for our sins and reconciled our hearts with God. He gave us His righteousness and empowered us with the Holy Spirit for our devoted service to God. Jesus also mandated believers to continue the ministry of intercession to revive and save lost souls.

Revivals in the Old Testament

Spiritual decline and futility preceded most revivals in the Old Testament. God's people had a conditional covenant with Him to serve Him only. Yet, after the time of Moses and Joshua, Israel was unfaithful to God. The Levitical priests failed as intercessors, so Israel stumbled deeper into sin and rebelled against God's laws by worshipping idols. Also, Israel sacrificed their children to these gods. They often blended godly and ungodly service in search of prosperity and comfort. Hence, they faced challenges; famine destroyed their wealth, and the Philistines, Midianites, Assyrians, and Babylonians conquered them. Thus, Israel encountered spiritual decline, moral darkness, and misery, as God withdrew His presence and scattered them among the nations. However, the merciful Lord sent prophets and judges such as Samuel, Othniel, Ehud, Shamgar, Deborah, Barak, Joel, Nehemiah, and Elijah to intercede for the revival of Israel. They led them to repent from their sins, restoring worship and prosperity. God gave them the pattern that brought revival to His people.

> *"13If I shut up heaven that there be no rain, or if I command the locusts to devour the land, or if I send pestilence among my people; 14If my people, which are called by my name, shall humble themselves, and pray, and seek my face, and turn from their wicked ways; then will I hear from heaven, and will forgive their sin, and will heal their land." — 2 Chronicles 7:14*

Thus, the Old Testament intercession for revival included the repentance and confession of sin, fasting, destruction of idols, cleansing, rededication of the temple and holy vessels, and the commitment to devoted worship. Then, God hears, forgives, and heals, restoring joy and prosperity.

153

Confession and Repentance

The word of God commands a confession of sin and an acknowledgment to God and the neighbor we have sinned against. It is an essential part of our walk with God as humans. God requires us to be aware of our sins as fallible humans, turn from those sins, and do better with His help (Leviticus 16:21; Nehemiah 9; Ezra 9:5-15; Daniel 9:3-12).

Sin is the only barrier that separates man from God. So, when God made a covenant with Israel, He also showed them the way to revival when they disobeyed. God said true repentance is the first step to revival. So, he revealed the people's sins to intercessors and guided them to repentance. For instance, God told Joel why the cankerworm and the caterpillar had eaten their blessings; and showed them the way to restoration. When they confessed their sins, God restored them. Also, intercessors proclaimed God's laws to the people and led them to repent. For example, when Ezra read the laws to the people, they acknowledged and confessed their sins while weeping.

> *"If I shut up heaven that there be no rain, or if I command the locusts to devour the land, or if I send pestilence among my people; If my people, which are called by my name, shall humble themselves, and pray, and seek my face, and turn from their wicked ways; then will I hear from heaven, and will forgive their sin, and will heal their land."* — **2 Chronicles 7:13-14**

Thus, with knowledge of the laws, intercessors defined the specific violation, led confession, appealed to God's mercy, and stopped their evil ways. Then, the people surrendered to the Sovereign God and obeyed His commandments.

Prayer and Fasting

In the Old Testament, prayer and fasting were part of the revival process. For example, God made fasting mandatory on the Day of Atonement, a day the high priest stood in the gap for God's mercy for Israel. Similarly, all the revivals led by kings, judges, priests, and prophets involved fasting. For instance, Daniel fasted while praying for the restoration of Israel from captivity. Likewise, God told Joel to declare a fast when their enemies destroyed their crops and property.

> *"Also on the tenth day of this seventh month there shall be a day of atonement: it shall be an holy convocation unto you; and ye shall afflict your souls, and offer an offering made by fire unto the LORD." — Leviticus 23:27*

Furthermore, God told the Israelites to show mercy to the poor during fasting, so He will answer their prayers (Joel 1:14).

> *"⁶Is not this the fast that I have chosen? to loose the bands of wickedness, to undo the heavy burdens, and to let the oppressed go free, and that ye break every yoke? ⁷Is it not to deal thy bread to the hungry, and that thou bring the poor that are cast out to thy house? when thou seest the naked, that thou cover him; and that thou hide not thyself from thine own flesh? ⁸Then shall thy light break forth as the morning, and thine health shall spring forth speedily: and thy righteousness shall go before thee; the glory of the LORD shall be thy rereward."*
> *— Isaiah 58:6-8*

We must recognize God's sovereignty by devoting seasons of fasting and prayer to humble ourselves in the sight of God. We must also confess our sins and depend on God to restore us during fasting.

Corruption by our sins makes us unclean, and all our righteousness becomes filthy. Thus, He hides His face from us because of our iniquities. So, we fade as leaves, and our iniquities, like the wind, have taken us away. Therefore, we must call on God to stir Himself to take hold of us. He promises "our light breaks forth as the morning, and our health shall spring forth speedily: and our righteousness shall go before us; His glory shall be our reward." (Isaiah 58:6-8).

Destruction of Idols

Worshipping anything other than God is idolatry. It leads to defilement and takes away His glory. So, when the serpent beguiled Eve, enticing her to become like God, the couple defiled themselves, lost the glory of God, and became naked. Also, God told Jacob to destroy all the idols in his household before restoration. More so, the first commandment of the Ten that God gave Israel was:

"Thou shalt have no other gods before Me."

The first sin the Israelites committed was idolatry at Mount Sinai. As a result, Moses destroyed the golden calf and asked for God's mercy on the people. God always commanded His people to cleanse themselves of idols before He visited them (Genesis 35:2). The holy God cannot dwell with uncleanness. So, God's presence left the Temple when Israel brought idols into the sanctuary. Thus, intercessors led the cleansing of the Temple to restore true worship. Godly kings such as Hezekiah and Josiah led Israel to rid the Temple of idols (2 Chronicles 29:3-31:21; 2 Kings 22-23). There is also a record of Temple-cleansing by Nehemiah (Nehemiah 13:4-14), and that of Josiah (2 Kings 22-23). Idols profaned the Temple and misused the holy vessels, resulting in obligatory purification. They put down the idolatrous priests and their altars in Israel to focus on God.

Rededication

Israel built the Tabernacle and Temple and dedicated these holy places of worship to God. It became a national identity for ancient Israel. However, God's presence deserted the building when they worshipped idols, something against the laws of the covenant. For revivals to restore the genuine worship of God, godly priests cleansed the sanctuary and rededicated it to God. They also rededicated themselves to the Lord.

> *"And at the dedication of the wall of Jerusalem they sought the Levites out of all their places, to bring them to Jerusalem, to keep the dedication with gladness, both with thanksgivings, and with singing, with cymbals, psalteries, and with harps." — **Nehemiah 12:27***

> *"And the priests and the Levites purified themselves, and purified the people, and the gates, and the wall." - **Neh. 12:30***

After the rededication of the Temple, the priests led the people to resume worship with daily and seasonal sacrifices and offerings, which attracted God's presence. Thus, revival reinstated the offerings and sacrifices as required by the law. Repentance and consecration to God led to wholehearted, genuine worship of the living God. Genuine worship restored their relationship with God.

Reward

Then God heard their prayers and had mercy on them. He forgave and cleansed them from their sins; restoring their land. God protected them from destruction and restored joy. God's salvation and righteousness brought joy through the reconciliation of their relationship. Restoration requires God's favor, forgiveness, and forbearance.

God created man in His likeness. He endowed him with life qualities of harmony. However, the Fall and its consequences perverted these gifts. Sin ruined the relationship between God and man. Sin always brought separation, misery, pain, and destruction to man. God initiated the plan of salvation to restore and give humanity a probationary period to conform to His image. God's law covers all dimensions of life. He instructs all men to remember Him and foster healthy relationships. God promises a life of peace, wholeness, and happiness to those who follow His laws.

Examples of Revivals in the Old Testament

- Moses and Israel — Exodus 4:18-31
- Othniel — Judges 1:12-27
- Ehud — Judges 3:1-31
- Deborah — Judges 4-5
- Gideon — Judges 6
- Samson — Judges 13:1-16
- Samuel and Israel — 1 Sam 7:1-13
- King David and Israel — 2 Sam 24:1-25
- King Solomon — 2 Chronicles 6
- Asa — 2 Chronicles 15:1-15
- Joash and Josiah — 2 Chronicles 34-35
- Jonah and Nineveh —Jonah 1-4
- Hezekiah — 2 Chronicles 29-31
- Ezra — 5-6
- Nehemiah — 8-10
- Daniel 9

Moses and Israel's Revival

After God delivered the Israelites from Egypt, they encamped at Mount Sinai while Moses ascended the mountain to commune with God for forty days. Israel assumed Moses died in his long absence, so they coerced Aaron to make an idol for them to worship (Exodus 32:1). Aaron took gold from the people and created a golden calf. The people declared the calf led them from Egypt (Exodus 32:4). They sacrificed to the idol amid their celebrations and sexual immorality.

Moses descended from the mountain and saw their abominations. He got angry and threw down the stone tablets inscribed by God, breaking them (Exodus 32:19). Thus, God declared His intention to destroy them and use Moses to start a new nation. Moses, however, began interceding on behalf of Israel, asking God for forgiveness and restoration of peace.

> *"Thus I fell down before the LORD forty days and forty nights, as I fell down at the first; because the LORD had said he would destroy you.[26] I prayed therefore unto the LORD, and said, O Lord GOD, destroy not thy people and thine inheritance, which thou have redeemed through thy greatness, which thou hast brought forth out of Egypt with a mighty hand.[27] Remember thy servants, Abraham, Isaac, and Jacob; look not unto the stubbornness of this people, nor to their wickedness, nor to their sin:[28] Lest the land whence thou broughtest us out say, Because the LORD was not able to bring them into the land which he promised them, and because he hated them, he hath brought them out to slay them in the wilderness."* —
> ***Deuteronomy 9:25-28***

After that, Moses destroyed the idol and punished those who willfully sinned. First, he reprimanded Aaron and asked, "What have these people done to you that you have led them into such evil?" The second outcome of God's wrath was on unrepentant leaders who refuse to humble themselves in shame and deliberately flaunt their opposition to Him. Finally, in response to a call from Moses for supporters against immorality and idolatry, the Levites stood at his side. Afterward, Moses ordered the Levites to kill everyone who refused to humble themselves in repentance, and they slew 3,000 there.

Moses then returned to the mountain for the people (Exodus 32:30). Besides the slain 3,000 who blatantly rebelled, the Lord also sent a plague as an additional punishment. God threatened to take His presence from among them and let an angel lead them. As Moses pleaded with God not to abandon them, God heard Moses' prayer and granted his wish.

All things are visible to God. Even before Moses descended from the mountain, God had already seen the sinfulness that had overcome the people (Exodus 32:7-8). Sin will bring God's wrath to people, and atonement is required (Galatians 6:7). Moses met with God three times after Israel's sinful behavior to forgive their sins and requested that God not take His presence away from them.

Yet continuing in willful, unrepentant lifestyles can remove God's favor from a person - no answer to prayers, mercy, protection, and presence of God will be turned away (Isaiah 59:1-2; Jeremiah 18:17). Humility, prayer, and confession are necessary for forgiveness. God delights in showing mercy. Genuine confession in humility of forgiveness and restoration.

The Revival of Joshua and Israel

Joshua was faithful to God when Moses sent him and the other eleven spies to check the Promised Land. He succeeded Moses as Israel's leader. God had said that he would give the land to him. So, Joshua and his men crossed the river Jordan and entered Canaan. They drove out the nations that previously dwelled there and took possession of the land there.

Furthermore, Joshua lived the land and wanted his nation to continue to serve God until his death at 110 years. Thus, he assembled Israelites and their leaders before the Lord and recounted how God had led and blessed them abundantly, fulfilling His promises based on fearing and serving God and putting away abominable gods. Though others still forsook God's statutes and commandments and worshiped idols, he commanded them to put those strange gods away.

> *"Now, therefore, fear the LORD, serve Him in sincerity and in truth, and put away the gods which your fathers served on the other side of the River and in Egypt. Serve the LORD! But if you refuse to serve the Lord, then choose today whom you will serve. Would you prefer the gods your ancestors served beyond the Euphrates? Or will it be the gods of the Amorites in whose land you now live? But as for me and my family, we will serve the Lord."—**Joshua 24:14-15***

We must side with Joshua to serve the Lord. As led the people to renew their covenant with God. It is also important as we gathered to confess our sins and turn from our personal and corporate sins, recognizing God's holiness and renewing fellowship with Him.

Revival with Prophet Samuel in Israel

Israel grew unfaithful to God during Samuel's reign. They worshiped Ashtaroth of the Canaanites. Samuel showed Israel how they had failed from the commandments God gave to Moses. He said to all the Israelites,

> *"If you are returning to the Lord with all your hearts, then rid yourselves of the foreign gods and the Ashtoreth and commit yourselves to the Lord and serve him only, and he will deliver you." — 1 Samuel 7:3*

Samuel prevailed upon the Israelites to get rid of all idols and worship and serve God alone. After many oppressions from the Philistines, Israel realized their need for God.

- They went to Mizpah, drew water, and poured it unto God. On that day, they fasted and confessed their unfaithfulness to God.

- After that, they destroyed all the idols that inhibited their acknowledgment of the only true and living God.

> *"Assemble all Israel at Mizpah, and I will intercede with the Lord for you. He also said, As for me, God forbid that I should sin against the Lord in ceasing to pray for you. Ceasing from prayer is a sin against God." — 1 Samuel 7:5*

Samuel made a sacrificial offering to God to secure Israel's pardon and interceded for the people at Mizpah. He also prayed for Israel during the war that defeated the Philistines, recapturing the Philistines' land. After that, Samuel served as the leader of Israel at Mizpah (1 Samuel 7:1-11). Therefore, persistent prayer and confession are essential during revival to return to God.

Prophet Elijah's Revival

After Solomon's demise, Israel was divided into two kingdoms. Judah and Israel each ruled by a different king. When the Northern Kingdom of Israel rebelled against God with idolatry, Elijah pronounced a drought on the nation for three and a half years. Israel, inspired by King Ahab and Queen Jezebel, worshiped Baal, their fertility and rain god, which were part of the surrounding culture. After three years, Elijah called a burned offering contest between him and the prophets of Baal, so it would determine who they should worship.

After God performed a miracle through Elijah on Mount Carmel, the people declared their stand for God, and Elijah led them to kill all the prophets of Baal. God showed His superiority over the prophets of Baal, as Elijah displayed the power of God when he prayed, and fire from heaven consumed the sacrifice, which the prophets of Baal could not do. Israel fell to its knees and worshiped God.

> *"37Hear me, O LORD, hear me, that this people may know that thou art the LORD God, and that thou hast turned their heart back again. 38Then the fire of the LORD fell, and consumed the burnt sacrifice, and the wood, and the stones, and the dust, and licked up the water that was in the trench. 39And when all the people saw it, they fell on their faces: and they said, The LORD, he is the God; the LORD, he is the God." — 1 **Kings 18:37-39**

Israel repented of following Baal and declared that Israel's God is the only God. Finally, Israel restored the true worship of God and rain was abundant. God often allows challenging situations to help us identify our weaknesses and rely on Him.

King Asa's Revival and Moral Change

Asa, the third king of Judah, was a man of integrity. His rule marked a revival in the worship of God. Asa sought the word of God and rededicated the vessels to the house of God.

> *"Asa commanded Judah to seek the LORD, the God of their fathers, and to keep the law and the commandment. He also took out of all the cities of Judah the high places and the incense altars. And the kingdom had rest under him."* — **2 Chronicles 14:4-5**

- King Asa dismantled the centers of idolatry that Solomon had established in his later years to appease his foreign wives.
- He led the people to obey God's laws and commandments. Judah rebuilt its city under his leadership.
- The Lord blessed, guided, and gave him security with prolonged periods of peace and prosperity. God made him victorious in wars (2 Chronicles 14).

Subsequently, he trusted in human help in a battle and relied on doctors to heal his infirmity. He took the treasures from the temple and gave them to the king of Syria for his protection from the king of Israel. We must not seek man's help or give God's glory to man.

We must not allow success and deceptive easy lifestyles to influence us, nor let personal pursuit lead us away from the Lord.

King Jehoshaphat's Revival

Jehoshaphat ruled Judah after the death of his father, Asa. He depended on God, unlike previous kings who sought the help of foreign gods such as Baal. Jehoshaphat removed places of worship of foreign gods such as Asherah poles. Jehoshaphat followed David's example at the beginning of his reign, so the Lord was with him. The Lord secured his kingdom, and he became wealthy and respected.

- God's fear fell on surrounding nations, causing them not to consider war with him (2 Chronicles 17:10).
- The Philistines, the enemies of Israel and Judah, brought him gifts and silver as a tribute. The Arabs also brought him 7,700 rams and 7,700 goats (2 Chronicles 17:11).
- He enhanced military security with the building of fortresses throughout the land (2 Chronicles 17:12-13).
- He had troops numbered and stationed in fortified towns throughout Judah (2 Chronicles 17:14-19).

When surrounded by his enemies of four powerful nations, he declared a fast, and the people called on God for help. God answered their prayers and defeated the enemies that came against Judah (2 Chronicles 20). The people took four days to gather the spoils from their enemies.

After that, Judah enjoyed peace and prosperity. Jehoshaphat displeased God when he made alliances with the kings of Israel who did not serve God. We should seek God's counsel, wait on Him, and not on resources for our benefit that do not please Him.

King Josiah's Revival of Judah

King Josiah was Judah's last great king before the Babylonian captivity. Manasseh, his grandfather, had reigned for 55 years, leading the nation into idolatry. Manasseh worshipped idols, Molech. He shed and offered his sons in the fire as part of the worship ritual and filled Jerusalem with innocent blood (2 Kings 21:16).

So, God determined to send Judah to captivity because of Manasseh's wickedness. While in captivity, Manasseh repented of his wickedness close to the end of his life. God heard his prayer and mercifully allowed him to return to Jerusalem, where he tried to undo all his wrongs against God. Yet, Amon followed in his father's earlier pattern of evil, turning again to idolatry and reigned for just two years.

At eight years, Josiah became king, and he ruled in Jerusalem for thirty-one years. He served the Lord faithfully and followed the ways of David. In addition, he led the people to renovate the Temple.

When the High Priest found the Book of the Law in the Temple, he read it before Josiah. He was sorrowful when he heard what was in it because they had not followed it. So, he directed his elders to ask the Lord what was written in the law. When they went to see the prophetess Huldah, she told them God would bring disaster on Judah according to everything written in the book the king of Judah had read because of their sins. However, Huldah declared that God would not punish Judah during King Josiah's reign because he humbled himself before the Lord when he heard God's judgment.

Notwithstanding his favorable prophecy, Josiah summoned the elders and people into the Temple, and priests read the law to them. Then Josiah commissioned the people to restore the pact with God. It was to obey the laws He gave and serve God with all their well-being. After this confession, the priests and doorkeepers removed the Temple's idolatrous things, as commanded. Then, outside Jerusalem, he burned them in the Kidron Valley and brought the ashes to Bethel. As a result, they killed the priests who worshipped idols. Finally, he destroyed all the idolatrous things implanted in the presence of the people. From Gaba to Beersheba, Josiah brought everything back into the way God commanded it to be.

> *"Neither before nor after Josiah was there a king like him who turned to the Lord as he did—with all his heart and with all his soul and with all his strength, in accordance with all the Law of Moses." — **2 Kings 23:25***

After Egypt's king was on his way to fight Assyria, Josiah went to fight him, even though God told him not to do so. As a result of his disobedience, they killed Josiah in battle. They carried his body to Jerusalem and buried it.

Just as Josiah, an intercessor, surrendered on his knees and cried out for deep brokenness. We must fall with broken fellowship because of rebellion and lack of knowledge of God's sacred commandments (Amos 4:6). Revival begins with humility after seeking the Word and prayer. God expects His people to be humble before Him and turn away from their unrighteous lives. Repentance is God's grace that enables you to change the direction of your heart. Besides, God works graciously to guide men to repentance.

King Hezekiah and the Revival in Judah

King Hezekiah, Ahaz's son, was twenty-five years old when he became the king of Judah; he reigned in Jerusalem for twenty-nine years. He became king of Judah after the reigns of several kings who disobeyed God. A vast decline, injustice, and negligence toward God had taken place in Judah. He also took reign at the time; the invading armies had destroyed the northern kingdom of Israel. Nevertheless, he obeyed and did what was pleasing in the LORD's sight.

- He reopened the doors of God's Temple, which his father had closed.
- He summoned the priests and Levites to remove all the defiled things from the sanctuary. He warned their ancestors had been unfaithful and did what was evil in the sight of God. So they abandoned His dwelling place; they turned their backs on him. They ceased burning incense and burnt offerings at the sanctuary of the Temples' God. So the Lord made them objects of dread, horror, and ridicule.
- He also asked them to renew their covenant with the God of Israel so that his fierce anger would turn away from them.
- He reminded Judah not to neglect their duties any longer! Since the LORD had chosen them to stand in His presence, minister to Him, and lead the people in worship and present offerings to him. The Levites cleansed the Temple of the LORD, just as the king had commanded. He removed Judah's idols, pagan Temples, and altars. He replaced idolatrous things with those dedicated to God and Temple service.

Hezekiah summoned the city officials, went to the Temple of the Lord, and offered sacrifices to God. He then stationed the Levites at the

Temple of the LORD. Finally, he observed all the commands the Lord gave to King David through Gad, the king's seer, and the prophet Nathan. He also reinstated the sacrificial Passover celebration as a national holiday.

Also, he reestablished worship in the Temple. Thus, there was immense joy in the city, for Jerusalem had not seen a celebration like this one since the days of Solomon, King David's son. Then, the priests and Levites stood and blessed the people, and God heard their prayer from his holy dwelling in heaven. When they returned to God, they were prosperous. Thus, he also threw off the ruthless Assyrians who had defeated many nations and defeated the Philistines. He fortified Jerusalem's walls against the siege.

Hezekiah found success in whatever he did because, while obeying, God was with him. He followed God and restored the service for Him. He led the people of Judah through a period of inward and outward revival, having only hope and passion for God.

However, because he boastfully showed his possessions to the Assyrians, God warned him they would carry those possessions away.

Thus, we must learn not to boast or forget the Lord in times of blessing (2 Kings 16-21, 2 Chronicles 28-33).

Prophet Jonah and the national Revival of Nineveh

God commissioned Jonah to preach repentance to Nineveh, although the Ninevites were hostile towards Israel. However, he went to Tarshish instead of Nineveh because he knew God would show mercy to them if they repented. Unfortunately, a terrible storm occurred in the middle of his voyage, and the shippers' cast lost and found Jonah guilty of their disaster. Therefore, Jonah confessed his guilt, and the mariners threw him overboard and asked God to forgive them.

> *"We pray, O Lord, please do not let us perish for this man's life, and do not charge us with innocent blood; for You, O Lord, have done as it pleased You."—Jonah 1:14*

God got Jonah's attention when a whale swallowed him up. Inside the whale, he had a personal revival and reconciled with God. Jonah remained inside the whale for three days and cried out to God.

> *"I cried out to the Lord because of my affliction, And He answered me. Out of the belly of Sheol I cried, And You heard my voice. For You cast me into the deep, Into the heart of the seas, And the floods surrounded me; All Your billows and Your waves passed over me Then I said, 'I have been cast out of Your sight, Yet I will look again toward Your holy Temple.' The waters surrounded me, even to my soul; The deep closed around me; Weeds were wrapped around my head. I went down to the moorings of the mountains; The earth with its bars closed behind me forever; Yet You have brought up my life from the pit, O Lord, my God. — Jonah 2:2*

After acknowledging his rebellion, He accepted God's discipline and repented. After that, Jonah was given another opportunity to deliver the Word of God to Nineveh (Jonah 3:2). This, Jonah went and faithfully proclaimed the word of God, saying,

> *"Forty more days and Nineveh will be overturned."* — ***Jonah 3:4***

When the King of Nineveh heard God's judgment, he called for national repentance and fasting for God's mercy. The Ninevites fasted and repented, and God forgave their sins and showed them mercy. But Jonah became angry, hoping for disaster. He wanted the city punished for its wickedness. Afterward, he sat outside the city, awaiting the destruction that never came. However, the city repented when they heard the Word, which shows that God's heart goes out to the lost people in sin. God will forgive the repentant sinner, but Jonah did not have the heart to rejoice over the salvation of the people of Nineveh. An earthly father would have replaced Jonah with another person who was a willing person to take His message, but not our Heavenly Father.

Though Jonah attempted to escape the mission, God never left him. So, we must do God's will when He commissions us. He can use unpleasant situations to call people to repentance. Prayer is an essential part of our life. God is merciful and does not play favoritism. We must be glad when people repent, knowing God is in control and is more interested in developing our character.

> *"**And he** prayed unto the LORD, and said, I pray thee, O LORD, was not this my saying, when I was yet in my country? Therefore, I fled before unto Tarshish: for I knew that thou art a gracious God, and merciful, slow to anger, and of great kindness, and repentest thee of the evil."* — ***Jonah 4:2***

171

Joel and the Revival of Judah

Prophet Joel was the prophet of Judah during the reign of king Joash. He proclaimed God's message of imminent disaster and judgment for sin, and His decision to strike the kingdom of Judah without warning. Dark clouds would descend on the lands with locusts and strip every living green thing within hours. Nevertheless, God told them to blow the trumpet, sanctify a fast, and call for a solemn assembly during a crisis. He directed them to repent and fast for His salvation.

Men needed to repent as judgment drew near; Judah needed to reconcile her heart with God. The heart of God's people is where revival begins. God desired them to surrender their lives and wills to Him completely. A revival occurred when the people repented and humbled themselves with prayers and fasting (Joel 1:13-14).

> *"Therefore, also now, saith the Lord, turn ye even to me with all your heart, and with fasting, and with weeping, and with mourning: And rend your heart, and not your garments, and turn unto the Lord your God: for he is gracious and merciful, slow to anger, and of great kindness, and repented him of the evil. Who knoweth if he will return and repent, and leave a blessing behind him; even a meat offering and a drink offering unto the Lord your God? Blow the trumpet in Zion, sanctify a fast, call a solemn assembly: — Joel 2:12-15*

The people ended their garments as an outward sign of grief and sorrow. However, it was more for show than for genuine sorrow. God was not interested in rituals but in the heart (Psalm 139:23-24). Thus, God promised them kindness, victory over the enemy, boldness, fruitfulness, joy, blessings, abundance, and restoration of honor.

God promised them the Holy Spirit, which He fulfilled when God poured out His Spirit on the disciples on Pentecost (Acts 2). The Lord is mindful of those who seek Him. Those who desire Him will find Him. God is interested in blessing His people bountifully. During this day of the Lord, God will destroy His enemies, but bring unmatched blessings to those who faithfully obey Him.

We must remind ourselves of His goodness, mercy, presence, and compassion. God wants us to stop our disobedience. Since He is Holy, we must also be holy.

Nehemiah, Ezra, and the Word Revival of Judah

Seventy years after the Babylonians destroyed the Temple in Jerusalem, Governor Zerubbabel, together with godly people such as Nehemiah, rebuilt the Temple. Nehemiah also rebuilt the city walls and played an essential role in spiritual rebirth. Subsequently, Ezra led a spiritual revival when gathered all the Israelite and read the law to them (Nehemiah 8:9-11).

He led the people to repent after narrating how God made a covenant with Abraham, delivered Israel from Egypt, and gave them the land of Canaan. Ezra also recounted how Israel had been unfaithful to God despite His goodness and compassion (Ezra 9:3). Thus, the people rededicated themselves to serve the Lord (Nehemiah 8, 9, 10).

God does not forget His promises, but some of His promises are conditional. For instance, the promise of restoration, healing, forgiveness, and blessing depends on humbly seeking God's face in repentance. Ezra appealed to the promises made by the covenant-keeping God. As intercessors, you must be mindful of God's past deeds and His faithfulness to act powerfully at the right time. Thus, revival begins in our hearts when we repent of our rebellion.

173

Haggai and Revival

In the book of Haggai, it displeased God that the people stopped the Temple work and began building their own houses, saying, "The time does not come, the time that the Lord's house should be built" (Haggai 1:2). This caused God's blessings to cease. However, when Haggai prophesied and encouraged the people, they continued the Temple work as God empowered them. As a result, God promised them His peace and greater glory than before (Haggai 2:1-23).

Zechariah

In Zechariah's visions, the enemy resisted Joshua, the high priest, because he was filthy. Nevertheless, God changed his clothes and forgave him. However, they would need to rely on God to finish the Temple. Zechariah also prophesied that Zerubbabel would complete the Temple construction he started. Further, God encouraged him not to despise small beginnings but to obey God's word (Zec 4:7-10).

Revivals in the New Testament

God delivered Israel frequently from sin and bondage. But they continued to rebel and mock His mercies often. Thus, all the revivals in the Old Testament were short-lived. The people often returned to their wickedness after enjoying freedom for a while. Most especially after the intercessor died; therefore, these revivals did not restore full fellowship between the people and God. There was a continuous cycle of decline and renewal among God's people (Judges 2:10-19). Israel eventually suffered a period of spiritual dryness with no open revelations, either through prophecy, visions, or dreams. There were no leaders except the Pharisees, who led dry spiritual lives and led many astray. Besides, the Sadducees denied the power of God and believed in rituals. However, there was hope for a redeemer. The Old

Testament intercessors, who were a foretaste of the ultimate intercessor, foretold Christ's coming. These prophecies inspired intercessors like Simeon and Anna to pray for their fulfillment. God ordained John the Baptist as the forerunner to prepare the way before Christ (Mal 3:1-3; Isaiah 40:3-5).

John The Baptist and Revival

The prophet Malachi foretold the ministry of John the Baptist. Later, God sent Angel Gabriel to tell John's father, Zechariah, that God had heard his prayers, and he and his wife Elizabeth, old and barren, would have a son named John. John will be a great man for the Lord. As a Nazarene, he will never drink wine or beer. Even before he is born, he will be filled with the Holy Spirit. He will help many people of Israel return to the Lord their God. John himself will go ahead of Jesus and make people ready for his coming. He will be powerful like Elijah and will have the same spirit. He will make peace between fathers and their children. He will cause people who are not obeying God to change.

John had to live a restricted and austere life during his preparation. He lived in isolation in the desert for most of his life. Nevertheless, he boldly preached the uncompromising word of God, focusing on repentance. John the Baptist preached God's judgment in Israel for disobedience and improper service to God. He performed no miracles (John 10:41), but John's revival manifested in the following ways:

- Preached Confession and Repentance of Sin.
- Baptism in water.
- Proclaimed Jesus as the Messiah.
- Commitment - Worship of God through Jesus.
- Return to obey God's law.
- The result brings joy and prosperity.

So, the Jews from Jerusalem and Judea went to hear John's words. He baptized them in the Jordan River after they confessed their sins. The people revered him as a true prophet of God. He announced Jesus and always pointed people to Jesus, saying, "He that comes after me is mightier than I." (Matthew 3:11). People wanted to live obediently and were hungry for more of God. So, the multitude came to John and asked for counsel on what they should do for salvation, and he counseled them.

> *"Teacher," they asked, "what should we do?" "**Don't collect** **any more than you are required to**," he told them. Then some soldiers asked him, "And what should we do?" He replied, "Don't extort money and don't accuse people falsely—be content with your pay." — **Luke 3:13-14**

Jesus and Revival

Jesus remains the final revivalist who reunited man's heart with God. Before His arrival, John the Baptist preached that God's judgment on the world was imminent and that the people should repent for salvation. John baptized Jesus and later introduced Him as the Lamb of God that takes the sin of humanity. John also declared that God had entrusted everything to His son, Jesus.

Jesus gathered His disciples for His ministry of salvation after He triumphed over Satan's temptations. His ministry focused on spreading the gospel and showing God's loving nature to man, with healing and deliverance that brought great joy to the people. The people marveled at His new doctrine and gave God the glory for giving such power to man (Matthew 9:1-8).

*"But Jesus told them, I must preach the good news of the kingdom of God to the other towns as well, because that is why I was sent." — **Luke 4:43***

His ministry spread abroad, and enormous crowds followed Him wherever He went. He healed every sickness and cast out all demons. He preached in the synagogues throughout Galilee and Judea and cast out demons. Wealthy and influential religious leaders sought an audience with Jesus. However, the crowd following Jesus made it hard for people to get close to Him. His fame spread throughout the region with these miracles, and Pharisees wondered how the entire world had gone after Him.

At Samaria: While Jesus and His disciples were traveling through Samaria to Galilee, He encountered a Samaritan woman that led to the revival in the city called Sychar. While his disciples went to the town of Sychar to buy food about noonday, Jesus sat by Jacob's well, tired from the journey, and a Samaritan woman came to the well to draw water. Jews had traditionally loathed Samaritans for years, so the woman was surprised that Jesus asked her for water. He further revealed her ungodly lifestyle, and she perceived Him as a prophet. Jesus taught her true worship, saying God desires those who worship Him in spirit and truth. She left her vessel at the well and returned to the city, bringing many people to meet Jesus. When the inhabitants of Samaria also heard Jesus' message, they believed in Him. They asked Him to stay with them, and Jesus stayed with them for a few days.

*"[28] The woman then left her waterpot and went her way into the city, and saith to the men,[29] Come, see a man, which told me all things that ever I did: is not this the Christ?" — **John 4:28-29***

177

The Apostles' mission: Jesus taught His disciples and gave them the authority to heal others in His name. He sent out the apostles to preach the kingdom of God, heal the sick, and cast out demons. He also empowered seventy other disciples, who went as an advanced team to all the places he planned to visit. The disciples returned from their mission and reported to Jesus the miraculous works they did for the people. But Jesus cautioned they should instead rejoice because their names are in heaven.

> *"17And the seventy returned again with joy, saying, Lord, even the devils are subject unto us through thy name. 18And he said unto them, I beheld Satan as lightning fall from heaven. Behold, I give unto you power to tread on serpents and scorpions, and over all the power of the enemy: and nothing shall by any means hurt you. Notwithstanding in this rejoice not, that the spirits are subject unto you; but rather rejoice, because your names are written in heaven." — Luke 10:17-20*

Ultimate Revival

God's ultimate revival for humanity occurred when Christ died on the cross for sins and reconciled us to God. The place of His unconditional love and selfless sacrifice to the fallen undeserving sinners.

> *"In this is love, not that we loved God, but that He loved us and sent His Son to be the propitiation for our sins," — 1 John 4:10*

On the Cross, Jesus Christ, the Lamb of God, offered to atone for our sins through His sacrifice (1 John 2:2). God's wrath is against all our ungodliness and unrighteousness, for the wages of our sins and rebellion to God is death. Jesus took and bore all our sins,

178

condemnation, and the consequences of our sins. The Holy son satisfied the condition and offered humanity full pardon and everlasting life. Man is helpless and cannot earn God's love or acceptance by self-righteousness or effort because we are all like unclean things, and all our righteousness is like filthy rags. Thus, He bridged the gap between the Holy God and sinful man through forgiveness, mercy, and peace.

Furthermore, when Jesus had His last breath on the cross, darkness fell, the earth shook, rocks split, and the dead were resurrected. He defeated the devil and took dominion over hell. Through this, He defeated the power of sin in our lives (1 John 3:16).

Consequently, He released humanity from the bondage of Sin and Satan. The curse of the law was destroyed at the Cross and the power of sin over us was broken, and the old sinful nature was snuffed out at the Cross-releasing God's mercy, forgiveness, healing, deliverance, and blessing to man.

The Holy Spirit and Revival

Joel prophesied the outpouring of the Holy Spirit on all flesh in the last days (Joel 2:28-32). John the Baptist baptized the Jews with water to forgive sins. But he told Israel Jesus would baptize them with the Holy Ghost and with fire." (Matthew 3:11).

After His resurrection, Jesus told His not to leave Jerusalem until the Father sent His promise, which Jesus said was a baptism with the Holy Spirit for empowerment to accomplish His mission worldwide So, on the Day of Pentecost, a day Israel celebrated the first fruits of the wheat harvest 50 days after the celebration of Passover, when many disciples were praying, the Spirit came upon them (Acts 1:4-5, 2:33).

*"¹And when the day of Pentecost was fully come, they were all with one accord in one place. ²And suddenly there came a sound from heaven as of a rushing mighty wind, and it filled all the house where they were sitting. ³And there appeared unto them cloven tongues like as of fire, and it sat upon each of them. ⁴And they were all filled with the Holy Ghost, and began to speak with other tongues, as the Spirit gave them utterance." — **Acts 2:1-4***

While speaking in other tongues, devout Jews, and other men from other nations, could understand them in their foreign languages (Acts 2:6). This miraculous sign amazed some people, while others mocked them as drunks (Acts 2:13-14). Then, filled with the Holy Spirit, Peter talked about Christ and addressed salvation to the crowd. After this, the people repented truthfully from their hearts. That day, they won about three thousand people over to Christ. Also, believers develop a passion for souls with a deep concern for the lost. Intercessory prayer has a tremendous impact on evangelism. Peter's sermon was profoundly different after they received the Holy Spirit. His preaching pierced their hearts and brought forth an immediate response from the crowd. About three thousand people were saved and baptized that day (Acts 2:37-42).

"Therefore let all the house of Israel know assuredly, that God hath made that same Jesus, whom ye have crucified, both Lord and Christ. ³⁷Now when they heard this, they were pricked in their heart, and said unto Peter and to the rest of the apostles, Men, and brethren, what shall we do? ³⁸Then Peter said unto them, Repent, and be baptized every one of you in the name of Jesus Christ for the remission of sins, and

ye shall receive the gift of the Holy Ghost. ³⁹ *For the promise is unto you, and to your children, and to all that are afar off, even as many as the Lord our God shall call.* ⁴⁰*And with many other words did he testify and exhort, saying, Save yourselves from this untoward generation.* ⁴¹*Then they that gladly received his word were baptized: and the same day there were added unto them about three thousand souls.* ⁴²*And they continued steadfastly in the apostles' doctrine and fellowship, and in breaking of bread, and in prayers."*. — *Acts 2:36-42*

Afterward, they talked about the beautiful things God had done as they helped spread the Gospel worldwide. The revival spread throughout the Roman Empire, among Jews and Gentiles, despite severe persecution from multiple groups: Jewish people, religious leaders, and pagans.

Philip's Revival at Samaria

The revival in Samaria was part of the mandate Jesus gave the disciples to spread the gospel, beginning in Jerusalem, Judea, then to Samaria and the uttermost part of the world. Besides, the persecution of believers contributed immensely to the spreading of the gospel. The persecution in Jerusalem precipitated Philip's movement to Samaria to preach the gospel. The people prepared when Philip arrived with his message. God confirmed Philip's preaching with signs and wonders. One sorcerer, Simon, got converted and subsequently baptized.

"For unclean spirits, crying with a loud voice, came out of many that were possessed with them: and many taken with palsies, and that were lame, were healed. And there was great joy in that city." — *Acts 8:7-8*

181

The apostles in Jerusalem sent Peter and John to Samaria when they were told Samaria had accepted the gospel. After arriving in Samaria, the apostles prayed for new believers to receive the Holy Spirit.

The Eunuch and Philip

Philip obeyed an angel and headed for a lonely desert road. The Holy Spirit asked him to join an Ethiopian Eunuch when he encountered him. Philip preached to the Eunuch who was reading the scriptures without understanding. He baptized the Eunuch after accepting Jesus as his Lord, and the Eunuch went away with joy. Philip found himself in the town of Azotus. He preached the gospel there and in every village along the coast, all the way to Caesarea (Acts 8:26-40).

Revival in Cornelius' House

When Cornelius saw a vision, he obeyed the angel's message from God. He immediately sent three men to tell Peter to come to his home. Cornelius gathered his household and acquaintances to hear Peter's message in anticipation of their return with Peter. God also told Peter to go to Cornelius, though he was a Gentile. After the initial formalities between Peter and Cornelius, the Holy Spirit descended on all who listened to Peter as he preached the gospel of Christ. He stayed for several days, teaching and spread the life and ministry of Jesus. Cornelius and his people became believers (Acts 10:1-48).

Paul and the revival of the Gentiles

Paul and other disciples, such as Barnabas, Silas, John Mark, Luke, and Timothy, embarked on missionary journeys that brought revival to the Jews and Gentiles in Antioch, Athens, Corinth, Ephesus, Iconium, and many other cities. For instance, there was a great revival in a jail in Philippi, as Paul and Silas praised God in their predicament. The authorities jailed them for praying for a demon-possessed lady whose masters made money from her divination. The masters were furious because they had lost their livelihood from the lady's divinations. So, they reported Paul and Silas to the magistrate, who put them in jail. But as Paul and Silas prayed and praised God at midnight, God caused an earthquake, and all the prison doors opened. The keeper of the jail, fearing that the prisoners had escaped, tried to kill himself, but Paul assured him they were all there. Then, he asked how he could be saved, and after Paul had preached, he and his household believed (Acts 16:16-34).

However, Paul suffered many persecutions for preaching the gospel. For instance, in Lystra, Paul and Barnabas prayed for a disabled person, but some Jews instigated the people to stone Paul dragged him out of the city, supposing he was dead (Acts 14:9-28).

The need for Intercessors

The world continues to tamper with God's creation, including godly values established by the Lord for our benefit. We have departed from God's standards He set for humanity.

The Bible says, in the last days, the love of many shall wax cold, and humans will be covetous and boastful, traitors, heady and high-minded blasphemers, rather than looking up to Christ. As a result, many will also depart from the faith. For instance, we have degraded the family system as instituted by God to suit our ungodly desires and wishes. Society has devalued the human body created in the image of God with all kinds of ungodliness. Sadly, we call it enlightenment. Also, man has degraded God's creation because of greed and power. Water bodies, vegetation, and the air have been polluted in our quest for more wealth and power. People are perishing without hope. But there is hope and peace when we accept Christ into our hearts. God grants mercy when we repent. Without repentance, there can be no revival. Also, there is no remission of sins and eternal life for those alienated from God. Reliance on flesh and human understanding without Christ does not yield empowerment from God.

Therefore, intercessors must rise and stand in the gap for revival in our societies. Revival will bring back those wandering away from the Lord. Family relationships can be restored, and church unity can be re-established by awakening society from apathy. Having the holy vessels of God intercede on our behalf without corruption brings renewed hope, faith, and a greater sense of unity and love. Amen!

Conclusion

Brethren, here we are, at the end of our journey of standing in the gap in place of prayer, petitioning God for His mercy to restore others; God had intervened through Jesus to restore communion. You learned that intercession is an initiation from God. He determines the conditions for intercessory prayers.

We made it abundantly clear that God poured out His abundant mercy and had already foreordained Jesus to stand in the gap in place of prayer before Adam and Eve rebelled in the Garden of Eden. Jesus had the mandate to plead for God's mercy, restore man amid misery and separation, and reconcile man to God. You also recall that before Jesus, God initiated intercession to restore the God-man relationship. So, He consecrated just a select few righteous men, such as Abraham, Moses, and the Levitical priesthood, who had the privilege of accessing His presence, atoning for sin, and praying for His people. However, some priests violated their agreements with God and performed their duties poorly. They mistreated their wives, widows, the fatherless, and the needy. Moreso, they oppressed strangers, denied justice, defrauded the people called to help, and became ineffective and God chastised them and honored those who obeyed.

When Jesus manifested in due time, He interceded by atoning for our sins on the cross and reconciling us to God. He also made every believer a priest. Therefore, it is a command for all men to pray without ceasing in the Spirit on all occasions, in contrast with the Old Testament, where only the chosen few had the mandate to pray to God.

Hence, intercession is still relevant to the body of Christ in contemporary Christian society. God restores faith in Him in challenging times when we intercede. Jesus paid the price for our redemption, but humanity is perishing in darkness. Thus, God desires us to rise and intercede for others. It grieves God when we neglect to pray for others. Intercession is a channel through which God releases blessings. God destroys the enemy's plan when we intercede.

Besides, God seeks intercessors today, since all believers in Christ have been drafted into the ministry of intercession. Thus, many intercessors prayed to God for the sake of people in history. The prophets, priests, Jesus, the Apostles, the early believers, and the church made intercessions. Therefore, all believers must stand in the gap and pray for others.

As today's believers and tomorrow's intercessors, you must stand in the gap in prayer for others. We have the Holy Spirit as our helper to come before God's throne, repenting and confessing our sins, asking for forgiveness for the communities in humility.

Furthermore, intercessors must be vessels of honor who possess godly traits. God always sets the standard for His servants, since none can approach the Holy God with uncleanliness. As a result, He consecrates and anoints men to honor Him. He also desires a humble heart, obedience, and faithfulness in worship. The Levitical priests had godly characteristics, yet they exhibited flaws.

But the ultimate intercessor, Jesus, was the only perfect intercessor. He is also the sinless vessel who defeated Satan. Love, peace, compassion, patience, and obedience were qualities He exhibited in His earthly ministry. He has empowered every believer with the Spirit to live a holy life and bear spiritual fruits.

Prayer has principles, so priesthoods with intercessory roles had a prayer model. God provided Moses with the model for all of Israel's priesthood in the Old Testament. The priests had the mandate to minister before God with sacrifices and offerings. The high priest stood in the gap and atoned for the sins of uncleanness in the Temple. Nevertheless, the animal blood sacrifice could not cleanse the priests and Israel from unrighteousness.

Thus, Jesus, the eternal High Priest, washed humanity of its sins — something that the blood sacrifices of Levitical priests could not offer. He gave them the agency to live in God's presence, offer spiritual sacrifices of praise, and enjoy an intimate fellowship with Him. Jesus satisfied all these requirements in the New Testament when He atoned for the sins of humanity and himself with his blood. Jesus became the great High Priest and the ultimate intercessor. He imputed his righteousness to all believers and gave a perfect model of prayer, which encompasses praise, confession of sin, thanksgiving, and private supplication, following the promptings of the Holy Spirit according to predetermination.

As man's greatest blessing, prayer must receive answers devoid of hindrances such as idolatry, disobedience, unbelief, extortion, ungodly family life, impatience, offenses, and unconfessed sin. We also noted that some Old Testament priests showed no reverence to God by offering imperfect sacrifices and maltreating their wives, and the less privileged in their midst, so they were not effective intercessors. Jesus, the High Priest, and the ultimate intercessor, obeyed God and received answers to His prayers. Jesus warned His disciples about the condemnable sins such as unbelief, offense, and many others that render prayers unanswered. Therefore, these identified hindrances must be confessed and eliminated.

We also espouse revival. As the Bible says, these last days, the love of many shall wax cold, and humans will be covetous and boasted. They will be despisers of good, traitors, heady and high-minded blasphemers, interested in their own lives, proud of their physical achievements rather than looking up to Christ. They will also depart from the faith. Further, many more people have the form of godliness but deny the power.

Moreover, a guide on intercession means we must all arise and be specific in confession and repentance, preparing our hearts for the move of God's Spirit in prayer. However, reliance on flesh and human understanding without holiness and purity does not yield empowerment from God. We must earnestly pray for the accurate proclamation of scriptures with the full power of the Spirit for our souls. We intercede for everyone according to God's heart. Intercessors must plead for boldness to proclaim the Word because empowered souls bring revival and power. God's purpose is to fulfill His vessels with holy courage, fervent prayer, and scripture. We can bring those who have wandered away back into the Lord's fold. Society can be awakened from apathy and restore family relationships and church unity.

God bless you for reading this book. I hope you enjoyed it. Remember to put the lessons you have learned into practice. Amen.

ABOUT THE AUTHOR

Henry R. Darko is a born-again Christian who believes that Jesus has restored man's fellowship with the Father by allowing him to be approved by God through His son. He is ardent about teaching the love of God to help people transform their lives. He is also the author of the book The Enemy Inside.

He holds a B. Sc. degree in Mathematics from Kwame Nkrumah University of Science and Technology, Kumasi, Ghana. In addition, he earned his BSc Ing. (Computer Science and Communication Engineering) and MSc. Ing (Computer Science and Communication Engineering, Major in Communication Engineering). Degrees from the University of Duisburg-Essen, Duisburg, Germany.

He has offered his services at the Tamale Technical University, Tamale Ghana, Social Security and National Insurance Trust Ghana, Makita Wurzburg, Duisburg, Germany, and Philips Priv-ID, Eindhoven, Netherlands.

His message dwells on the importance of intercession in these last days or end times and God's requirements for effective intervention. Furthermore, it defines intercessory prayers, intercessors, and their qualities and discusses how to intercede. It also highlights how to eliminate the hindrances to prayers and the benefits of intercession for God's glory.

Henry R. Darko is now a servant of the Almighty. As a member of the body of Christ, he has served and ministered in various capacities. He is blessed with the company of his wife, Ama, and children. Additionally, he is passionate about teaching and intercession.